NOT CARING WHAT OTHER PEOPLE THINK IS A SUPERPOWER

INSIGHTS FROM A HEAVYWEIGHT BOXER

ED LATIMORE

Edward.latimore@gmail.com

First Printing, 2017

ISBN 13: 978-1542628808

www.edlatimore.com

Contents

What This Book Is, How It Came To Be and Thanks

So this is a book. What I aim to accomplish with this book is to take what I have learned the hard way and give it to you so that you can learn it the easy way. I believe this is the purpose of all books. We read the words of other people so that we can learn from their experiences. Within these pages, I have condensed my experiences on various topics that I not only feel passionate about but that I also feel are essential to growing and getting the most out of life.

While I am incredibly proud of this book, I can not take credit for the original idea. At the start of 2015, twitter user IllimitableMan gave me a great compliment and suggestion. He told me that my twitter feed was great and that I should make a book of my best tweets. I liked the idea, but I wanted to do more than compile pages of 140 character blocks of wisdom. So I modified the idea. I took my best tweets, broke them down by category, and wrote an essay giving an in-depth treatment to each one. Where appropriate, I also followed the essay with an actionable step to help you apply the idea in your daily life.

I'd like to think I would have eventually come up with the idea for a book like this, but IllimitableMan gave me the original spark and has been incredibly encouraging throughout the whole process. I can attribute a great deal of my audience to exposure from him.

One night while working on my book, I got a message from Nick Curry (the artist formerly known as Victor Pride). In the most polite way possible, he told me that the title and cover of my first book for sale was trash. In doing so he noted that it was a shame for me to have such a powerful twitter feed but then do something like title a book "Twitter Poems and Insights". He then gave me some suggestions and came up with a much better title. That title is the title of this book.

Before Nick volunteered his time and insight, another twitter user chimed in with a similar observation that got the wheels turning. TheArtfulMan has contributed art and insight to my website and book and I value his contributions greatly. Speaking of the website, my website wouldn't exist if it were not for Jon Persson. While he has nothing to do with this book directly, his attractive design has allowed me to capture your attention. While I think my words are great, people are visual creatures. Jon took care of that angle with my website.

I have to thank Desiree Sinkevich for taking time out of her extremely busy schedule to give me a round of proof-reading. She has not only loaned those talents to my book, but she has also been generous enough to edit some of my blog pieces as well. Likewise, Erin Rossiter gave her valuable time to editing the manuscript and making some key suggestions that I might have otherwise missed.

The cover photograph is the result of the excellent camera work of Shawn Eisler. The font and the cover design are all due to Matt Lawrence putting up with my constant revisions. Both of these men are true professionals and because of them, the book really jumps out and grabs attention. I think the content in the book is excellent, but their work will make people look inside who might not otherwise give it a second look.

My lovely partner, my biggest fan, and supporter, Anna Potier, has believed in me and in this project from the very beginning. She loaned her editing eyes and also cooked amazing meals that freed up my energy to focus on the task of writing. When I finished a passage of my book, my first thought was "How will this help someone reading?". My second thought was "How cool will Anna think it is that I wrote these dope ass words?"

And lastly, above all, I thank everyone who reads my website, follows me on social media or bought this book. I'd like to think I have great insights about the world, but they'd be useless without an audience to thank me, offer suggestions and insights, or sometimes outright argue with me because they disagree. I could not craft this book in an echo chamber and I wouldn't want to. In this way, supporters, haters and those who don't even know I exist are responsible for the wisdom I've tried to put in these pages.

How to Use This Book

Many readers of this book found me because of Twitter. I'm not the best at Twitter but based on my rate of growth and what I've been told (objective and subjective markers), I think I'm pretty good. This is because I recognize it as a powerful tool for connecting with people and distributing large amounts of value.

I believe that if you put beneficial things out in the universe, the universe will send beneficial things back to you. As a result of putting out useful or entertaining information on Twitter, I've made great connections. One of those connections is Twitter user "IllimitableMan". He gave me the original idea of putting my best tweets together in a book.

Once I got them together, I sorted them into categories: Hard Work, Paradigm Shift, Relationships, Self-Control, Standards, Strategy and Tactics and Time. Following each tweet, I wrote an essay giving each an in-depth treatment. Then, where appropriate, I gave an actionable step to reinforce the idea expressed in the tweet. Each actionable step is something that you can do right at this moment to see the effect of the ideas executed in your life.

There is also a section of poetry. These were all poems composed in Twitter. The character count limit of Twitter means that none of my poems could exceed 140 spaces. All of the poems in this book originally adhered to this limit. However, for book formatting purposes I added spaces and converted the two line poems to four lines.

While this is not adding characters, it does add an extra space because Twitter counts new lines as a character. This means that if you take some of the poems—as they are formatted—directly into Twitter, they may go over the limit by a character or two. Other than that, all poems were originally composed and shared on my twitter account.

There is no right way to read this book. It's a collection of meaningful essays centered around the topic of the chapter. When you need some insights on increasing your work ethic or self-control, you will skim the essays there. If you're feeling lost in your relationship, the essays in that section will give you guidance. While you can certainly read the book sequentially, it is by no means necessary to get value from it.

May this book bring you as much insight reading it as it gave me writing it.

Stuff You Should Know Before You Read

Disclaimer 1

I'm a man. If that wasn't obvious from the cover, I'm stating it clearly now. Most of my book applies to men and women, but my relationship advice is written from the perspective of a heterosexual man. I'm not a misogynist, homophobic or any of the other words one might think to describe a man writing from his own, non-inclusive perspective.

It is simply the perspective I know best as that as what I am. Women and homosexual men can certainly read it and gleam some insight into the heterosexual masculine mind if they so choose to. Nothing is vulgar, disrespectful or anything I wouldn't say to my mother. But the disclaimer is here so you know that section isn't for everyone. You have been warned.

Disclaimer 2

I recommended some physical activity in the book. While I certainly hope you do them, if you get hurt or die as a result of following any of it, it's not my fault. In case that wasn't official enough for you, here's the disclaimer in specific disclaimer language.

This book is not intended as a substitute for the medical advice of physicians. The reader should regularly consult a physician in matters relating to his/her health and particularly with respect to any symptoms that may require diagnosis or medical attention.

The information in this book is meant to supplement, not replace, proper (name your sport) training. Like any sport involving speed, equipment, balance and environmental factors, (this sport) poses some inherent risk. The authors and publisher advise readers to take full responsibility for their safety and know their limits. Before practicing the skills described in this book, be sure that your equipment is well maintained, and do not take risks beyond your level of experience, aptitude, training, and comfort level.

Disclaimer 3

I don't give any legal advice or recommendations on breaking any laws to get what you want. However, should you do something stupid and illegal and present this book as the reason for your stupidity, stop right there. I have a disclaimer for that. The following disclaimer also protects me should you decide that your interpretation of my advice leads you to make a dangerous or illegal decision.

This book is designed to provide information and motivation to our readers. It is sold with the understanding that the publisher is not engaged to render any type of psychological, legal, or any other kind of professional advice. The content of each article is the sole expression and opinion of its author, and not necessarily that of the publisher. No warranties or guarantees are expressed or implied by the publisher's choice to include any of the content in this volume. Neither the publisher nor the individual author(s) shall be liable for any

physical, psychological, emotional, financial, or commercial damages, including, but not limited to, special, incidental, consequential or other damages. Our views and rights are the same: You are responsible for your own choices, actions, and results.

Not Caring What Other People Think Is A Super Power

CHAPTER ONE

Hard Work

The single most important trait for success is Self-Discipline.
Everything else takes care of itself if you have this.

While the recipe for success has many ingredients, there is disagreement on the most important one. If you ask ten different people, you're likely to get ten different answers. Here, I make the case for self-discipline. No matter what you choose to do, there will always be an unpleasant component. It will be difficult and lack enjoyment, but all great things have a great price. The price must be paid in full, upfront, and there are no refunds--only wasted opportunity.

You can't pay by cash, check, or credit card. Hard-work and time are the only currency that success accepts. This is why self-discipline is the most important trait. During the moments you don't want to work because the difficulty is great or your exhaustion is severe, self-discipline is needed to carry you on. Self-discipline pushes you forward regardless of your momentary feelings.

Without it, you won't do what is needed. You likely won't even start. If you cannot force yourself to take action towards your goals, nothing else you do matters. This is why the single most important trait for success is self-discipline. Everything else takes care of itself if you have this.

Actionable Advice

Start a running routine with a pre-determined distance. It needs to challenge you but be within the range of what's possible. No matter how much pain you're in, finish at least three times a week.

Get out of bed no later than 5 am every day. You needn't be completely aware or awake, but your feet need to be on the ground moving you towards the start of your day. It doesn't matter how slow you move. All that matters is that you don't get back into bed.

Every day do something that makes you nervous. The nervousness normally holds you back but now, as long as it won't cause you physical harm, do it.

The most underrated talent is the ability to work your ass off.

The question "What is talent?" generates a predictable response. Most people think of talent as exceptional ability and innate skill. While it's agreed that you can improve your baseline level of ability, certain levels of performance are reserved for only the talented. However, when pursuing success, talent is a great asset but it is not a necessary condition.

If there is nothing special about your mind or body, you can always work hard. The ability to work your ass off is underrated as a talent because we consider talent unique, special, and largely unteachable. Either you have it or you don't. Maybe you do have a genetic tendency for taking on long, tedious work. Even if you don't, working your ass off is a learnable talent.

Working your ass off is valuable because very few people do it. Even at the highest level of competition, few have learned how to persist when faced with real challenges. It's similar to what smart kids eventually experience. They coast through their studies until they come up against something that isn't so easy to solve. Rather than double down their effort, many conclude they aren't talented enough to do the work. In contrast, the hard worker immediately starts on the unpleasant parts of the task and is determined to find a solution.

This attitude is rare at all levels. Everyone from a factory worker to a CEO wants to avoid the unpleasantness of a hard problem. If you can attack difficult things with gusto and a high pain tolerance, there will always be a well-compensated place for you in the world. The most underrated talent is the ability to work your ass off. Therefore, it is immensely valuable.

There's always a demand for people willing to do what others won't. People are obsessed with the idea of working smart and saving energy. Become obsessed with working hard. Be grateful when something doesn't come easily to you. It forces you to learn the value of hard work. When life becomes a battle of attrition, only those who have learned the value of hard work will be left standing.

Actionable Advice

Distance running is great for many things, but now add sprints to your routine. A routine of hill sprints or distance runs covering 100 meters is sufficient. It doesn't matter how fast you run them. Only that you run them with great energy.

Do a jigsaw puzzle. Jigsaw puzzles are a great way for you see the value of persistence and hard work applied over time. The solution is never obvious and most people give up before they complete them. This is why they are adored by the elderly, a population with an abundance of time and wisdom.

Forgive those that have wronged you. Especially if you aren't ready to. You may fail here, but the complete abolishment of your feelings isn't the point. The point is to apply the mentality of working your ass off to your emotions.

The difficulty of a task is irrelevant if it is essential to your success.

Once you know what needs to be done to get what you want, nothing else matters. The difficulty and duration of the task is irrelevant. The only question is "Can this be done faster or more efficiently?" How you feel about the task doesn't matter. Your energy level doesn't matter. The arguments you had or the people making fun of you don't matter. The only thing that is relevant is doing what you must to get what you want out of this life. Never forget: at the end of the day, no one cares about your desires but you. Either you make them happen or they never will.

People can't read minds. Even if they could, they would use it to make their own dreams a reality. Your dreams are, at best, a secondary concern to other people. This is why your dreams must be a primary concern to you. You can't count on help. You can't count on the path being easy. This is fine because anything worth having never comes easy. If it's essential to your success, it's guaranteed to be difficult to obtain.

Actionable Advice

Pick a distance you would normally drive but walk it instead. Make sure it's to an important place and with a deadline. The walk will be difficult but since you have to be there, you will make it.

You have within you a book. It may be fiction or non-fiction. It may be long or short. But you have within you a story that someone who also speaks your language will pay to read. Write this book. You may never sell it, but sit down and complete the idea from start to finish.

Tell someone with whom you disagreed with that they were right all along. Do not tell them your changed of heart is due to an exercise in this book. They must sincerely believe that your stance has change. In this way, you learn how to subjugate the need for being right in favor of harmony. It may be difficult to swallow your pride, but at times it may be necessary. This is small practice for doing emotionally difficult things that can lead to greater success.

You must be prepared to put in months and years of mediocre performance before you become world class at anything.

Having talent is great, but all it does is move you a little closer to the finish line. You still have to do the hard work of winning the race. Becoming world class--the level at which you are in the company of the greatest on the planet—gives the best chance of winning the race. The race is long and tiresome. Many runners, even with the head start of talent, do not make it to the finish line. Others have no head start. No matter how hard they work, they will never make it. Only a select few ever cross the finish line.

The race takes years and you can't see the finish line until you've passed it. This is what talent doesn't account for and why it often dies out undeveloped. Talent makes someone look great at first but eventually, they have to compete against others with talent as well. What separates the merely talented from those that produce results and gain accolades is putting in the work to improve their weaknesses instead of relying only on talent.

The race never actually ends. You just get to the point where you and a few select people are the only ones still running. Those not willing to put in the work dropped out of the race many miles ago. Now the only competitors left in the field are those with talent and work ethic.

Maybe there's someone still sticking around with exceptional talent, but they'll drop out because of the hard work required to keep up. The untalented that have made it to this point because of hard work will run until the end but never take the lead. The talented who work hard will lead the pack. But to get to this point in the race, where only the world class remain, years of non-world class performance is necessary.

Actionable Advice

If you haven't already, pick something you want to excel in. Commit to practicing a little every day. Eliminate other distractions. While it doesn't need to be the focus of your entire life, you want to develop an appreciation for the commitment it takes to greatly improve your ability at something.

Discipline is freedom.

The idea of discipline seems restrictive if you lack understanding of human nature. People prefer the path of least resistance to their main priorities--a means to survive and reproductive opportunities. We take the easiest path to the most money (or the things it can buy) and sex (or the feelings that sex can provide).

If pursued without discipline, we consume in excess and without restraint. Living life in this way causes great suffering. Your health will deteriorate from an over-indulgent diet. You will prefer pornography or low-quality mates. A life like this makes you a slave to your impulses and the side effects of surrendering to them.

Discipline keeps your basic urges under control, enabling you to enjoy a higher quality of life. Relationships improve because you won't settle for the first person that satisfies your sexual appetite. You'll enjoy more of life because your health isn't a liability. You choose what to enjoy instead of being a slave to impulse. The only way to live free is to remain disciplined in the pursuit of a superior life. Discipline is freedom.

Actionable Advice:

Take a picture of yourself before changing to a high fat and high protein/low carbohydrate diet. Then compare the photo after thirty days of an exercise routine following this diet. Take note of your feelings and the reaction people have to you. You will look and feel better, giving you more opportunities in every area of your life. The more options you have in life, the greater freedom you have.

Learn how to order your favorite Chinese food in Chinese (or any language really, but there is an abundance of Chinese restaurants). It will be difficult and require discipline but upon mastering that, you will experience a few things. Sometimes you'll score a discount. Sometimes people in line will be impressed with you and this opens up a conversation. The confidence you develop will make you feel as if your mind can do anything.

When unexpectedly forced to wait--like in a traffic jam —don't express feelings of frustration. You are not expected to extinguish your feelings--only to temporarily smother them. This disciplines you to have control over the expression of the emotion before you attempt to actually control the emotion. You must walk before you can crawl.

Good pain comes from pushing towards a goal. Bad pain comes from avoiding challenges. Gonna suffer either way. Might as well become better.

Pain is inevitable. It's part of life. Not all pain is caused by the same thing but all discomfort is something you'd rather avoid. Everyone wishes they could avoid the pain of heart-break or of losing a loved one, just as they wish they could avoid the soreness after a workout or the embarrassment following a loss. The outcome--pain--is the same but the process of getting there is dramatically different.

This is the difference between outcome and process focus. A painful outcome is the result of tragedy or avoidance. This is the pain caused by a break-up or the loss of someone dear. This is the pain we should actively seek to avoid. The problem is when we confuse outcomes with processes. If we seek to avoid the pain of a process, then we never push our bodies and minds to something greater. That's because the process of self-development is painful.

Achievement results in an outcome superior to your present situation. Avoidance results in an outcome inferior to your past situation. Goal achievement is a painful process with a pleasant outcome. Avoiding a vital task is a pleasant process with a painful outcome. If you're going to suffer no matter what, you might as well be better for it.

Actionable Advice

Whatever number of repetitions you planned to do for an exercise, do an extra one. Even if--and especially--

you're in pain already. This is the pain of growth. This is the good pain that you must learn to push yourself through. You should not always push through pain like this, but doing it occasionally makes you better able to physically push through difficult things.

Whatever mental task you take on, gradually increase the amount of time you spend engaged in it. If you're studying or practicing, go five minutes longer once you feel you want to quit. You want to get used to engaging in constructive suffering. Muhammed Ali once said that he "only counted the sit ups once they started hurting." This is the same idea. You only count the time once you feel discomfort. This is when you learn how to embrace the pain of a process.

You can either choose to apologize first to someone that you have a disagreement with or you can approach a stranger randomly and strike up a conversation. Both activities will have the desired effect of forcing you to push through a painful process to reach a superior outcome. Typically, these are things that people avoid (because the process is painful) so they suffer an inferior outcome (deteriorated relationship or continued loneliness).

Do what you love and every day you'll work harder than the last.

Consider the hallmarks of love: devotion, patience, endurance, and happiness. If you do something you love, you approach it with the same traits. This ensures that you will work the hardest when you're passions are engaged.

However, one must be careful and consider the full implication of this statement. With the exception of your parents, everything you love in this world is a result of your time and effort. The time invested into relationships creates the love between you and the people in them. Your love of an activity grows as you invest time and energy into it. You do not fall in love with something before making an investment into it. The love of anything only comes after you have put in time and energy.

This is the greatest secret of all. Any skill you develop even a small proficiency in has the capacity to make you fall in love. Searching for something you love is a mistake rooted in misunderstanding. What you're really looking for is something in which you can have an initial success. This initial success inspires you to spend more time with the skill. After spending time building on your initial success and improving, you may suddenly find yourself in love.

Doing what you love drives you to improve. The energy expended doesn't exhaust you because you love the work you're doing. You work harder every day, thus giving you more reasons to love what you're doing. You can use this concept to develop a love for anything. Find something you love and you'll work harder than you ever believed you could.

Actionable Advice

Select something that you seriously dislike. This can be a physical or mental discipline. Examine your level of proficiency. You will likely find an inverse relationship between your dislike of something and your ability at it. You will find a way to improve so that you can experience a small amount of love for the subject.

Perhaps it is using a tutorial to solve a calculus problem, shaving fifteen seconds off your mile run, or telling a small joke to get people to laugh. This small success will change your attitude towards things you believe you don't enjoy. The goal isn't for you to suddenly fall in love with a new hobby. If that happens, it's a wonderful benefit. The main goal is for you to experience a small emotional shift in the direction of something that you once found tedious.

Every long term pleasure requires short term struggle and pain.
If you try to avoid the initial struggle, you'll suffer in the long term.

Shortcuts only shorten your preparation time. You'll still have to face the challenge and it doesn't care how ready you are. If you avoid the necessary hard work then you will not have the strength, wisdom, and ability to meet the inevitable challenges you'll face.

There are no shortcuts to anything worth having. Whether you do it sooner or later, you have to put the work in. However, if you do it later, you'll have a lot more to put in. The extra work comes from mental anguish of compressing a task into a shorter amount of time.

Shortchanging yourself will put you in a position to suffer more than necessary because it puts you at the mercy of the time. If you avoid the initial struggle, you'll suffer in the long term.

Actionable Advice:

When working on your craft, do not allow interruptions except for extreme emergencies. If you decide to work out but you forgot your water, continue working out. If you wanted to write but you forgot to pull up a key document, keep writing.

The point is for you to experience the pain of ill preparation. This need not be done often, but intentionally forgetting something vital to a process will increase the likelihood of you remembering it at another time. The pain of inconvenience will serve as a constant reminder you of the price you pay for putting off what is necessary.

Pain is temporary. Being a bitch that quits is forever.

No matter how severe the discomfort you experience, it eventually ends. Either you die or the situation improves. Therefore, quitting because of pain is not only foolish but cowardly. The pain, no matter how miserable, will cease one way or the other. You'll either perish or succeed.

Since you're experiencing pain anyway, you might as well finish and get a reward for it. The shame and cowardice from quitting will last a lifetime and forever echo in people's memory of you. Cowards truly die a thousand deaths.

Actionable Advice

When you start a new venture, undertake it with the mentality that you'll either succeed or die. Quitting is no longer an option. This is the only way that I have gotten as far as I have (with much further to go, mind you) in boxing and my studies. I do not accept quitting as an option. I will have to fail out. This is effectively death. This is how you must undertake all new endeavors.

You can have whatever you want if you earn it.

There's a price for everything. Sometimes it's monetary but most of the time it isn't. Money results from deliberate practice in a difficult and high demand skill. There are many ways to be rich but they all require the same thing from you. You can be rich in love, friendship, prestige, influence, respect, etc. It is simply a matter of applying deliberate practice in a different skill set.

It will be difficult, take time, and require work. The higher the value of your target, the more of these things it will require. But almost nothing is off limits. The only question is this: will you do what it takes to get what you want or will you retreat to lower hanging fruit?

Actionable advice

Understand that money is merely a fortunate side effect. Most of the things we value do not take cash or credit. Make a list of all the productive and desirable traits you have. Next, to this list, make a list of all your destructive and repulsive traits. Once you feel the list is as fully developed as possible, deliberately work on reducing your negative traits.

It doesn't matter how fast or how long it takes because you are increasing your value. Value building is a lifelong process. The more productive and attractive traits you have, the more likely you are to reach success. The longer your destructive list, the bigger liability you are to yourself.

The best view comes after the hardest climb.

Everything in life feels better if you've worked for it. The world feels better to you after you've contributed to it. The greater the exertion, the greater the joy felt at its completion.

A life full of easy and simple tasks can't be a meaningful life. We find happiness in things that push us to the brink of our abilities and force us to grow. This is because happiness is not a destination. It's a journey. You can come in third place in a race with tremendous effort or simply be declared the winner without taking a single step. Which one of these situations makes you feel better about yourself?

Actionable Advice

Make it a point to fill your life with challenging tasks. Build relationships that hold you to a higher standard. Keep your mind and body engaged in activities that push it to the limit. Only in a state of perpetual challenge can you experience happiness. The higher the climb, the harder it is. The harder the climb, the better the view.

Not only is success hard to attain but it is fleeting and has to constantly be re-earned.

The greatest enemy of future success is previous success. It's easy to forget how much work it took to reach the top once you've arrived. An incredible danger all successful people face is becoming addicted to the fruits of their labor to the point of neglecting the labor altogether. While one must find time to enjoy the results of their hard work, this cannot become a priority if they wish to remain successful.

Thermodynamics teaches us that all systems move towards disorder. The more complex the system, the more rapidly it descends into disorder unless energy is put into maintaining it. Your success is a complex system and like all systems, it obeys this rule. If you aren't putting energy into the system, the system will deteriorate. Once your success system deteriorates, then it becomes incapable of producing results.

The system has many moving parts and intricacies, but you know them intimately. This is your system so you know exactly where and when you need to put energy to maintain consistent output. As long as you take care of your success machine, it will take care of you. The machine must constantly be maintained. Success constantly has to be re-earned.

Actionable Advice:

Select a relationship in your life. The nature of the relationship is not important. It can be professional, familial, platonic, romantic, etc. Let the person know how much you value them and their contribution to your life. The reason you are doing this is so that you can understand the power of maintaining a system.

People often take relationships for granted so this is the easiest place to see the immediate effect of adding energy to the system. In re-earning the adoration, trust, and respect of someone with whom you have a relationship, you counteract the entropy in an important system in your life.

Some limits are real. Some limits are imagined. You won't know the difference 'til you try to push past them.

There are some things you can't do. Then there are things that seem like you can't do them, but it's only an illusion. The illusion is that they are impossible but the reality is that they are merely difficult. The only way to tell the difference between what is impossible and what is merely difficult is to put forth an intense and earnest effort.

The beauty of this approach is that even if you lack the requisite abilities to overcome the impossible, the attempt will develop you in many other ways. It's like the saying: "If you shoot for the moon and miss, you will still land amongst the stars."

You can't tell how deep the pool is just by looking at it. You can't tell just by wading in the shallow end. You must dive in head first at the deep end to truly know. You can make a good guess about the depth, but you can't know until you try to get to the bottom. Your limits are like this. You can't tell which ones are real or imagined until you try to push past them.

Actionable Advice

This piece of actionable advice requires you be in decent physical condition. It will apply to 99% of the population. If you're in the 1% of high-level distance athletes, congratulations. For everyone else, run five miles with no more preparation than a simple stretch. If you're a great runner already, swim one mile without any preparation.

Your limits aren't real. You have the ability to push past them by force of will alone. These distances seem far. They seem impossible. But even moving slowly, you can get them done and prove to yourself that they aren't impossible; only difficult. The impossibility you once perceived is merely an illusion that will evaporate once you apply pressure.

You are capable of far more than you know.

If forced to choose between what's best and what's safest, the people closest to you want you to take the safer route. This makes sense when you consider that they care deeply for you. What's safe is not necessarily fulfilling, but it does provide certainty to the social circle you belong to. This is why your ideas for bold action are rarely met with the enthusiasm and support you believe those closest to you should have.

If you aren't careful, this attitude will infect you and cause you to alter the plans you set for yourself. You'll start to sell your dreams short. You stop believing you are able of achieving your desires. To keep a member of the tribe safe, other tribe members subconsciously (or in some cases, consciously) deflate their ambitious dreams. Though many times their apprehensions are motivated by love, you must never forget that you are capable of accomplishing anything.

Those closest to you may not understand and try to dissuade you, but the only way to find satisfaction is to go for your desires without reservation. Even if you fail, you will not die in a state of quiet desperation. Despite what some may have told you, you are capable of far more than you know.

Actionable Advice

You once had a dream that you gave up on. Unless you're in the 1%, you wanted to be a certain person and you have given up (completely or partially) on being that person. I should have written a book fifteen years ago and studied physics, but I let people around me remove my willingness to fail. I know this because even in elementary school I was writing stories and was fascinated by math.

Do a little bit of your original dream. If you have trouble remembering, think back to what you did for fun when you were ten years old. It doesn't matter what it was. Find some way to reconnect with the piece of you that died. Give that part of you a resurrection, even if it's brief. This may lead to new life paths and directions. At the very least, renewed vigor about daily life is almost certainly going to occur. This is never a bad thing.

Limits are meant to be conquered. Never define yourself by that which you will abolish, for in your moment of triumph you will cease to be.

Conquering limitations forces you to become a higher caliber person. Defining yourself by restriction means that you are only what you have not accomplished. You won't be the type of person that does something; rather, you'll be the type of person that does not do something.

If you are defined by limitation, you must also find a new identity when your limitation ceases to exist. Redefining oneself is great when you seek it intentionally, but many have found themselves lost when their barriers evaporate. Seek to define yourself by what you accomplish, not by what you can't.

Actionable Advice

We often have the incorrect reaction to the success of others. While most of us have the social acumen to not express jealousy or unsolicited criticism, we are not aware of the excuses we make to ourselves for not achieving something similar. We often see someone accomplish something and immediately think, "I could do that if only I didn't have [insert problem or obligation here]."

This is similar to defining yourself by a limitation. When you do this, it mentally reinforces the reasons why you won't succeed. Everyone has different obstacles they face. You are no different. What is different is that other people are succeeding in the face of their difficulties. Other people are not defining themselves by their limits.

When you hear of someone's success, take a moment to ponder how you could make this happen despite whatever limitation you perceive yourself to have. If there are no successful people near for you to practice on, read about people who have done something you'd like to. Figure out how you'd do it, despite whatever limitation you think you have.

If you notice, this exercise doesn't ask you to imagine a world where you don't have the limitation or obstacle. That's unrealistic and useless. This exercise is a prompt for you to formulate your own plan for improvement. We often don't even bother to set a goal because we get too focused on what obstacles exist. That ends with this exercise.

A life without pain is a life without reward.

Pain is inevitable. Pain is part of life. If you've managed to eliminate pain, then either you have conquered all problems in this life or you're dead. The former tends to occur with the wealthy, but even they have to deal with the pain that occurs via interpersonal relationships. Or, they resign themselves to extreme loneliness. This level of isolation is not only painful, but it forgoes the rewards gained from personal interaction.

The latter group no longer experience life. This is both figurative and literal. Upon touching death, you are beyond the point of pain. You are beyond the point of living as well. The pain that we try to avoid means that we avoid life. The best and worst things walk hand in hand. Avoiding one automatically forfeits your right to enjoy the other. Your life becomes such that you might as well be dead.

Actionable Advice

Improvement requires you to hurt yourself. By hurt, I mean that you must experience damage to your ego (or body) that you will interpret as pain. If you're a single person, force yourself to have a conversation with the next attractive person you see. It doesn't matter if the conversation goes well. All that matters is that you force yourself to do it. The confidence and sense of accomplishment you experience will be immense.

The same idea applies to physical development. The old saying of "pain is weakness leaving the body" is true. The strain you experience pushing yourself through a workout is painful, but the reward is greater health and confidence. If you don't currently workout, make this your new mantra. This is good pain that needs to be experienced in order to grow.

Who cares how you feel about something if it's necessary to your success.
Worry about your feelings when you finish.

No one enjoys difficult things. That's part of what makes them difficult. Anything necessary to your success will be difficult. If it were easy, then everyone would be successful. The activities essential to your success go against your basic desires as a human being.

The human being is remarkably lazy. It would like nothing more than to achieve its goals while conserving as much energy as possible. Once a person is fed, sheltered, and has a consistent (though not necessarily authentic) sexual outlet, there is no motivation to achieve more. To get more out of life requires greater effort, but people avoid expending effort once they are satisfied.

However, no one wants to be in their 30's, broke, overweight, scraping the bottom of the barrel for a lover they are embarrassed to be seen in public with. Therefore, you must embrace the difficult things with gusto. It doesn't matter if they are difficult. In order to have a better time in this short life, you can't consider the difficulty of a task; only consider what completing it will bring.

Actionable Advice

Become an early riser. Whatever time you currently wake up, start waking up an hour earlier. It will be unpleasant, but don't focus on that. Instead, focus on how you will use the time. You can work out, work on a project, study, or even just keep your home clean. The idea is that you learn to see the benefit of a difficult task instead of focusing only on the unpleasantness.

Be so good that people think you're cheating.

The highest compliment someone can pay you is to believe you aren't competing fairly when, in fact, you are. This type of advantage is the result of innate ability developed through hard work. Competition evaporates when you leverage your natural talents with hard work. When you're simply talented, people think your victories are the result of blessing. When you're a hard worker, they think your victories are the result of effort.

These scenarios don't enrage competitors because they can rationalize being out-worked or "out-blessed." The problem is when both forces align. People start to believe you are operating outside the rules. Your goal in life should be to operate in spheres where you have as much of an advantage as possible. The results of your hard work will be multiplied.

Make your competitors believe that you have not only divine blessing but divine work ethic as well. Make them believe that you couldn't possibly be playing by the rules. Be so good that people think you're cheating.

Actionable Advice

Learn to identify the markers of talent, hard work, and the vicious combination of both. Study people who perform outstandingly in their chosen craft. These people are hard workers but they also have a deep well of talent to draw upon. Your challenge is to look at the top performers in a field and decide how their ability is distributed. What portion of their success is hard work and what portion is talent?

You must also identify where you have a particular talent. Whether you decide to leverage your ability there is not so important at the moment. What is important is that you identify where you naturally accomplish more than others while putting in less time than them. There are many ways to do this, but I will tell you my favorite method. While not always fool-proof, you are likely to have an advantage in the things you enjoyed when you were 10 years old with fewer responsibilities.

I'm not talking about playing video games or reading books. Those don't require skill. Hopefully, you were interested in something that required skill, even if your skills in them were lacking at the time. For example, I loved writing stories and the only video games I liked playing were role playing games. I enjoyed those games for the story and the writing. Nearly 2 decades later, I still find myself writing and I look forward to doing much more of it. What you loved is likely to be where you now possess an advantage.

Laziness feels good now. Hard work feels good later.

Laziness is a short-term solution to discomfort. The future is always coming and is something we must be prepared for. The best preparation is to do the necessary work at the moment. Laziness is a way to prematurely experience the comfort that results from hard work. This comfort arises not only because of accomplishment but because of a lowered level of anxiety.

When you experience relief without doing the work to earn it, the reduced anxiety is short-lived. Deep down you know that you aren't really in a position to enjoy the comfort. You know that your work is still incomplete and that you'll be forced to return to it or suffer immensely. This is why the masses look forward to Friday and hate Monday. Throughout the week they do just enough to sustain discomfort and the weekend is their artificial sense of relief.

Working harder now lets you do more later. Eventually, those "laters" will be "nows." This is the secret to a prosperous life. Anything important to your future that can be done now should be done now. By putting it off, you're delaying the inevitable. During this delay, you cost yourself valuable time and increase stress. You end up wasting more time because it's likely that other important tasks accumulated in the background while you were procrastinating. Procrastination feels good now. Getting things done feels good later.

Actionable Advice

There is likely something that you have been putting off.

This is something important. It could be making an appointment, completing a workout, paying a bill or even cleaning up. Whatever you are putting off won't require much effort to identify. It will be the task that you immediately think about when you try to relax.

Instead of disappearing into the land of unearned comfort, take action and do the thing. This way, you'll feel good now. The comfort you experience will be earned because an important task is now complete.

Always believe that you can fail. Once you think you're invincible, you'll stop working hard and it will be your demise.

In your quest to become the best version of yourself, the only thing that will keep you vigilant is the belief that you won't make it. Many people mistakenly believe they have done enough when in reality, they're not even close. Complacency is bad enough, but it's even worse when you're prematurely complacent. The remedy for complacency is fear of failure.

Fear of failure is an interesting thing. It never goes away. One must learn to act in spite of it and use it to stay focused. Think of fear as the ground below the tightrope. There is the danger of falling but you still must cross. You must rely on focus and courage. These traits are at their best when the possibility of failure is at its highest. Survival instincts kick in. You become your best to face the worst. If you don't believe that you can fail, then these instincts will remain dormant and you will never achieve your potential.

Believing that you can fail is only one part of it. You must also believe that you are far from fulfilling your potential. This fear and this belief must be coupled with a genuine desire to be the best. When these ingredients come together, then you will put forth an extraordinary effort. If any of these ingredients are lacking, then you may start to believe you are invincible. This leads to complacency which will lead to your demise. Always believe that you can fail.

Actionable Advice

Approach everything you do as if you are struggling. There is a saying: approach what is hard as if it were easy and approach what is easy as if it were hard. This is the proper mindset for growth. If you approach difficult things as if they are easy, then you won't get discouraged with the challenges.

If you approach easy things as if they are difficult, you are less likely to make stupid mistakes that will lead to your demise. In all of your endeavors, take this approach and proceed with humility.

When you struggle through a problem, you get better.
The easy way now produces a hard way later.

Struggling through a problem--learning things the hard way--is the best way to learn. Solutions arrived at through struggles are deeply understood and possess greater depth because they are earned rather than given. You come to own and understand the solution.

If someone just tells you the solution, you might solve the problem in the short term but life is one long continuous problem. You will not further develop your actual problem solving ability. Solving specific problems increases your general problem-solving ability. This is a skill that make your life much easier, so every opportunity to improve it should be taken.

Actionable Advice

Choose a non-health or non-legal problem you have. You are to solve it without consulting the internet or other people. You must rely on your experience, grit, intuition, and trial & error to solve the problem. Do not give up. Whatever the problem is, you are committed to solving it without assistance. Though this method is not ideal for many problems you face, it will teach you a valuable lesson about struggle.

It may not even be ideal for the particular problem you've chosen. No matter what, it will sharpen and develop your problem-solving skills and build your confidence in them. In turn, you will be a better problem solver when you solve other problems with more resources at your disposal.

Not Caring What Other People Think Is A Super Power

Set some goals. Stay quiet about them. Get 'em done. Post results only.

Everyone loves the feeling of telling the world about an ambitious goal they're working on. Even before the age of social media, people announced to the world when they were about to do something big. Usually, people don't follow through with these goals. All they get is a short rush of attention.

Why don't they follow through? Maybe it's because the work is too hard or they lack the necessary resolve. At a deep level, they know this. But remember: the human being's natural tendency is to get as much as it can for as little effort as possible.

People want the rewards of the task without doing the actual task. They can't get the tangible rewards of completing a hard task so they settle for the next best thing. They get to experience the feeling of having many people curious about them and their plans. Instead of doing the actual work to become interesting, they make themselves appear to be in a constant state of business. However, nothing actually ever gets done.

The easiest way to hijack this tendency is to restrict the conversation to things you've done. This will train you to get your validation from actual accomplishment and not a possibility. Only discuss the results of your goals. There is a song lyric that perfectly sums this idea up: "And of course you can't become, if you only say what you woulda done."

Actionable Advice

From now on, only talk about the things that you have accomplished. Many people talk about their plans as a way to become interesting. From now on, you will accept being boring until you are actually interesting. You accept being a loser until you actually succeed.

You do not get to talk about anything you plan to do unless you have made a significant amount of progress towards that goal. But, even then, other people must broach the idea first. You are no longer at liberty to bring up any of your plans for the future. However, feel free to boast about anything that you've already accomplished.

Do what makes the most sense instead of what feels best, and you'll be in a better position to do whatever you want.

Taking the most sensible path is no guarantee of superstar success. However, it is better than acting only on feeling because it forces you to make disciplined, calculated moves that consider your resources and the future. When you act based on your emotional state, all you consider is the present and how to attain the specific emotion you want from the situation. Rarely does this work out in your favor.

Reacting emotionally will always leave you one step behind. This is because you'll still have to deal with problems you neglected in the midst of being emotional. The problems don't go anywhere just because you were preoccupied dealing with your feelings about the last problem. Taking a strategic, disciplined approach puts you in a better position to deal with future problems. This is important because there will always be future problems.

A reactive approach places you in a reactive position. The reactive position, by definition, is the position that is second to act. You will never be able to get ahead in life.
Acting sensibly now allows you to be free in the future. It allows you to be proactive. The proactive posture is one that grants you the ability to act first. Acting emotionally now is a path to enslavement later.

Actionable Advice

In many ways, this is related to harmful effects of

procrastination. Procrastination seeks relief by delaying work while the overly emotional seek relief by rushing through the decision. Ideally, one takes a while to make sound decisions but acts quickly upon them once the decision is made. It's a stressful process, but rushing through it in an emotional state greatly decreases the possibility of making a sound decision.

We wish to improve decision making. To improve your decision making, absorb the basic ideas behind probability and statistics by taking a class, watching a YouTube video or reading a book.

You need not become a math wizard, but you want to understand that some things are more likely to occur than others and that basing your decision on these likelihoods greatly increases your chance of success in life.

Opportunity follows struggle. It follows effort. It follows hard work. It doesn't come before.

If you understand the nature of opportunity, then you understand how to increase the amount you have. Opportunity does not choose people at random. However, it is impersonal and impartial. All sectors have opportunities but the only way to take advantage of them is to be an active participant in life.

Opportunity likes being taken advantage of. Opportunity wants to be ridden by a hustler. It's turned off by the lazy or the lame. Whether you have to seize opportunity or it is given to you, it will quickly desert you if you are not prepared to put in the work to keep it. Sometimes, the initial work for the opportunity is greater than what it takes to sustain it. Sometimes, it's less. But what is consistent is that the harder you work in your chosen sector, the more opportunity you have and the more you'll be able to get out of it.

Actionable Advice

There is something that you want in your life. It doesn't matter what it is but for the next 30 days, you must devote all of your spare time to acquiring it. This means putting in extra work, doing research, making sacrifices and doing many things that you haven't done before.

There is no guarantee that you will have what you want after 30 days but if you undertake this task with earnest effort then you will be a lot closer than you were a month before. You will be in a better position for opportunity to find you so that you can take advantage of it.

Not Caring What Other People Think Is A Super Power

A ritual or tradition may become so successful that you start to doubt if you still need it. This is the greatest danger of success.

The greatest danger to success is the life that success affords. When you're low on resources and high on wit, you make sound decisions because you have to be efficient. Efficient choices and disciplined behavior are good because they force you to plan and use strategic thinking.

When you have many resources--resources acquired from your wit and grit--you often forget how hard you had to work to attain them. Your abundance makes you comfortable. In comfort the oddest thing happens--you start to resent the hard work that allowed you to become comfortable in the first place.

This is why successful traditions deteriorate and those at the top may suddenly find themselves at the bottom. You must be vigilant against the threat that success brings. When one has everything they could want and the time to enjoy it, they often question why they should keep working so hard. This is the trap to avoid if you wish to remain sharp and competitive in your given craft.

Actionable Advice

There is an area in your life where you excel. Maybe you aren't better than most, but it is the area in your life in which you have the greatest proficiency. Because this is an area in which you have great proficiency, you've likely slacked off in the vigor with which you approach development. Over the next 30 days, to do something you haven't done before in this chosen area.

You are to push your limits and recall the feeling of improvement. Recall the eagerness of struggling to get better as a beginner and seek to recreate this with vigor. At the end of 30 days, you'll see the results of pushing yourself in an area where you were once content. The improvement in your abilities will remind you of what you are missing out on when you fall victim to the trappings of success.

Your life will be hard if you only make easy choices.

Think of all the people who have more money and better health than you. Think of all the people with fulfilling relationships and a greater amount of comfort than you. Once you eliminate the people that got lucky via the lottery or a windfall legal settlement, you see a correlation. Their lives are the result of discipline and sacrifice.

These things are difficult. Making money, staying in shape, and building constructive relationships are all more difficult than making minimum wage, eating terrible and not building friendships. When choosing between something that requires more effort and something that requires less, always go with the one that demands more. The rewards you reap will be in in exponential proportion to the effort required.

Actionable Advice

For the next week, experiment with a new diet. If you eat anything you want, eat a low-carb diet. If you're already low-carb, go vegetarian. If you're a vegetarian, you try veganism. If you're a vegan, try the raw food diet. If you live the raw food diet, I've got nothing for you—congratulations, you're a statistical outlier. Use the structure of this piece of actionable advice to create your own challenge.

The point here is to do something harder than your normal actions and to track any benefits you get. For some, there will be physical benefits and for some there won't. However, all will experience the mental and emotional clarity that comes from increasing discipline.

These are most important.

CHAPTER TWO
Self Control

Emotions are meant to add richness and depth to your life--IF you control them. But most people don't. So they bring ruin and despair instead.

Emotions serve a single purpose. They give meaning to an instant that would forever be lost with the passage of time. Most are unable to perfectly recall the details of a moment. Even if they could, there are many subtle nuances and experiences that give it meaning. Emotions allow us to encode the important parts of the experience in a format that is easily understood—how we feel.

The experience is encoded as an emotion because feelings are easier to recall than facts. This is the order of things—the details dictate the emotional reaction so we store the details through emotion. The problem arises when the order is reversed. You will experience tremendous confusion if you try to remember a feeling with details, and then try to recall your emotional state with only a recounting of facts.

When you do this, you attempt to make reality match your emotional state instead experiencing the depth of the emotion that reality brings. Trying to bend reality this way is a recipe for failure because reality doesn't care how you feel. You may have an interpretation of it, but if you are not aware of what this interpretation means then you are headed towards trouble.

Actionable Advice

Before you get angry, ask yourself what your anger will accomplish. The point of this question is not to dissipate your anger. There are many things in this world worth being angry about. The purpose of asking this question is to make you realize that while emotions may motivate you to do certain things, they themselves do not make anything happen.

We believe that if we get angry or sad enough, then something will happen to change reality. Unfortunately, this is very far from the truth. Your emotions allow you to experience the world in a way that makes it memorable and meaningful, but they do not alter it at all.

If you don't have control of yourself, you can't get control of anything else.

Here's a how to know what you actually control in your life: you only control something if you can guarantee that it will never be taken from you by time, force or preference. In other words, what do you have that will last forever, no force in this universe can take from you and cannot decide that it prefers to be with someone else? There is only one thing that fits that criteria—your intent.

You can exercise a large degree of influence over many things. An influence so strong that the illusion of control fools you. It's false. People can die. Plans change. Spouses leave you. The body can break down in unexpected ways. You can do all the right things and avoid all the risks in life, but still be in the wrong place at the wrong time. The only thing you really have control over is your intent and perspective. You get to choose where to place your effort and how you see things. Everything else is beyond your mortal grasp.

Actionable Advice

When people say that you only have control of yourself, it's slightly misleading. You don't even really have control over your body. You unexpectedly get sick. There may be lurking genetic diseases in your genome. All unexpected injuries and assaults represent the limits of your control. If you really had control over your body, then you would never allow it to fall under harm.

We do, however, control the mind. As far as technology has been developed, we are unable to alter another person's thoughts against their will. The actions may betray the thoughts when they take our suggestions, but it is impossible to actually change what a person thinks by any force of will.

When the world is going out of control, the mantra you will say to yourself is "The only thing I control in this world is my mind. Everything else can and will do as it pleases". Say it to start your day, say it to end your day, or say it when the day is not going according to plan. It doesn't matter what you say it, only that you say it until you internalize it.

The degree to which you can control the outcomes in your life determines your success.

Once you realize what you can control in life—your intent and your perspective—then you can focus on how to be successful. There are no guarantees. All you can do are things that increase your odds of success. When things don't go your way, pick yourself up and learn from them. Or stay down and sulk. This is a choice of intent and perspective.

By choosing to look at the hardships in your life as learning lessons, you are exercising control of your mind. When you learn from things, you increase your odds of experiencing success and happiness in life. You must control your mind so that you can force yourself to see things in a way that benefit you. The degree to which you can do this will determine your success.

Actionable Advice

You are no longer permitted to view anything in your life as a devastating or tragic event. From now on, everything is to be seen as a learning lesson. The way you do this is to start simple. No matter how terrible a situation is, ask yourself "What is positive about this?" Even the worst situation allows you to answer with, "I'm still alive."
 In
This shift of focus is an important step. It's difficult to learn if your mindset isn't properly aligned. Viewing the event as an education opportunity instead of a tragedy makes it less likely that you'll have to endure it again. This is because you can be on the lookout for ways to inoculate yourself against the unfortunate event if it

occurs again. However, if you only feel sorry for yourself then you will be scanning for pity and justification.

There is always something constructive about the moment that you can use to improve the quality of your life. The sooner that you do this, the better your life becomes. This is because effects are cumulative. Not only do you avoid more bad things because you are learning, but when tragedy does happen then you have practice responding to it in the correct manner. This means that you'll be quicker to see the lesson to be learned, and thus start learning them faster.

The only thing you can control is yourself and what you can influence is surprisingly limited.

The illusion of influence is interesting because there are some who argue that having influence IS a form of control. Assuming this is true, they make a logical continuation—if I have a small amount of influence there must be any number of things that I can do to have a larger amount of influence. A larger amount of influence means a larger degree of control. Therefore, it is possible to control things outside of myself.

This thinking is based on an erroneous premise. Control is not a gradient. It is binary. You either have control of something or you don't. You have control over some parts or you don't. If there are five valves that feed into one pipe that you have to turn and you can only turn 3, then you have control over three valves. You don't have 60% control over whatever they converge to. You have a small amount of influence on the flow controlled by the valves and that is it.

Though this is largely a semantical issue, it's an important one. Control is an extension of your intent, instantaneously causing a thing to act. Influence is merely a suggestion—albeit strong at times—that can be ignored. Anything that you can control can't be ignored.

Actionable Advice

When you want a person to do something for you, you have to influence them. If the difference between influence and control is still alluding you, imagine how frustrated you would feel doing a good job at a place for

10 years, asking for a raise and being told no.

Perhaps you deserved an increase in pay but you did not influence your boss properly. Imagine that you'd have to convince your boss to pay you more after 10 years of good service. Clearly, you can't force him so imagine what you do to influence his decision. Thinking about this problem in whatever context it's relevant to you will let you feel the difference between influencing and controlling a person.

The solution to 98% of your problems is "more money" or "more self-control". The rest are good problems. Or involve prison.

All problems in life are related to finances, health or relationships. The solution to all of these issues is either "more self-control" or "more money". Greater self-control allows you to conserve your finances, practice healthy habits and keep check of your emotions. If you have control, then you need to make more money so that you can afford better health care and a better quality of life. Improved quality of life improves the quality of people you are able to attract.

Most legal issues can be avoided with more self-control. If you're low on self-control, then you need to have a decent sum of money to hire a good lawyer. This gives you a chance to evade prison, but if your crime was particularly heinous (low self-control) or your lawyer was particularly bad (low amounts of money), then you are going to jail.

This is effectively the end of your life and is the most likely penalty for lacking control and funds. You either become homeless, in prison or dead. Of those three, the only problem that can't be fixed by "more money" or "more self-control" is death—and give that one another century or two.

Actionable Advice

Make a list of all the things you'd like to improve about your current life situation. On that list will be things that you can fix with discipline and hard work. There will also be things that can only be fixed with a greater income.

Generating a higher income will almost certainly be tied to improving the control you have over yourself and your moods. If you make enough money but you still have financial difficulties, you'll be solving your problems by controlling your budget and habits.

Customer service teaches you to keep your game face cool under pressure. It's a paid internship in emotional self-control.

To most people, customer service is a circle of hell. The people with customer service gigs working within elite sections of society may have a different experience, but the average person working at Starbucks or Walmart has their patience tested daily. I know this because I worked at Starbucks for 2 years and as a bank teller for 9 months.

These jobs are miserable because the average person is miserable and many of them take their frustration out on you. If you wish to remain employed, there's nothing you can do about it because your job is to serve the customer.

Your job is to endure any abuse that won't physically harm you because the goal is to keep customers that spend money. I think everyone should do a bid in a line of customer service. Here you will learn how to control your emotions, which is an immensely valuable skill. Learning to control your emotions is such a valuable skill because so few people can do it.

One of the best ways to get better at this is to be put in situations which force emotional control without the penalty of prison or loss of life. You learn how to swim best when thrown in the deepest part of the ocean. Or you drown. Customer service is like that. You learn to eat shit with a smile or you don't eat at all.

Actionable Advice

If you are able to or you aren't already employed there, I strongly recommended getting a part time job in customer service. Or working around children (if you have children, then carry on. Assuming you're doing even a halfway decent job, you're already more skilled than most).

If you have a problem controlling your emotional reactions, start your day with this mantra and say it whenever you need a reminder: "My emotional reaction will not only do nothing, it most likely will make my life worse." Prisons and cemeteries are full of people that had an emotional reaction but did not think of the consequences.

Control the mind first. The body will follow. Your mind will quit a thousand times before your body collapses.

Whenever I run, spar or write, there is always a point where I don't feel like doing it anymore. It's not that the work is exhausting, but rather it starts to bore me. We all have wanted to stop the hard work and do something else. The reason is irrelevant. What IS relevant is that you have control over your intent. The mind will quit a thousand times before the body breaks a sweat.

You can control what your body attempts to do. Your body will pass out and collapse before it dies so there is nothing to worry about. By controlling your intent, you control the part of yourself that waivers when you want to push your body. The body does not know what it is capable of doing—only the mind can know that. The mind is where intent lies.

Therefore, by controlling your mind, you control your intent and control your body. The body is dumb so it thinks that because of a little lactic acid build up, or side cramps or heavy breathing that it's about to die. The mind and intent know better, so it must control the body that wants to quit. Mental discipline will give you the ability to endure anything.

Actionable Advice

The running challenge is the best way to demonstrate this principle at play. I maintain that anyone of reasonable health can go out and run 6 miles with nothing more than a stretch and a warm up. It will feel miserable if you aren't in shape, but you can complete it.

Even if you do it at an incredibly slow pace, you will eventually cross the finish line. Your mind will want you to stop because of the discomforts, but you must control your intent and push through it.

Social media has more control over people than people have control over it.

Social media is addictive because it's one of the few places where a person faces no immediate repercussion for emotional over-indulgence. This is the nature of the internet and impersonal communication. The same reason social media is addictive is the same reason why guys think it's ok to send dick pics to girls via online dating apps. With no immediate repercussion, a person is free to indulge in whatever feels good at the moment.

Social media infects your mind by giving you constant access to a willing audience. This almost always leads to an over-inflated sense of importance. An exaggerated sense of entitlement always seduces and destroys. You will never have control over the social media mediums because you don't want control. You want to drown in the self-importance and lack of boundaries on social media. This is how it gets control of you—it gives you your biggest fantasy: it makes you the center of attention while simultaneously freeing you from negative consequences.

Actionable Advice

It was not too long ago that we did not have social media and its propagation over wireless networks. Many people feel their lives are connected via social media, but this is only a persistent illusion. To challenge this illusion, decrease your usage one level.

If you're constantly using, reduce your posting time to certain portions of the day. If you post intermittently throughout the day, don't post for a few days. The goal is to gradually increase the amount of control you have over social media.

We don't want to quit cold turkey because extremes of this nature won't work for most people. If you can completely eliminate using social media then this is excellent, but the gradual approach of increasing control is ideal and most likely to lead to sustainable success.

Control your emotions or they'll control you.

This is the crux of it all. Your emotions serve a purpose. They give feeling to things so that you may retain their meaning. If you do not control your emotions, they may lead towards actions that have disastrous outcomes. Trying to make the world match your emotional state instead of responding to the world with proper emotions leads to failure. This manner of living is very addictive and must be avoided at all costs. Control your emotions of your emotions will control you.

Actionable Advice

Operate under the assumption that the world does not care how you feel about anything. Maybe there are a few select people that care, but most in the world are only interested in what you can do for them and the value you bring. Being emotionally draining and reactive reduces the value you add to the world.

This is because people have their own problems to worry about and to assume they'll care about your problems is selfish. Not only will you repel others but you'll enrage yourself because the world will not respond to you the way you believe it should. Operate from the assumption that no one cares. This will allow you to make decisions that generate loyalty and care from other people.

Don't blame your failures on things you CAN'T control until you've maxed out on things you CAN control.

You cannot control your height, skin color, gender or where you were born. In the lottery that is the selection of those traits, some people end up with clear advantages that make the game of life easier. Others start at a marked disadvantage. However, the moment you decide to blame your misfortune as an adult on these things, then you deliver a grave insult to those that have succeeded with the same "disadvantage".

When you are at the top of the game, with the same skill sets and ability as someone else and you're STILL losing, then you have a case for some type of discrimination or societal limitation. Until then you simply do not measure up.

Actionable Advice

When people give you an excuse for why they couldn't do something, listen carefully, for you have an opportunity to learn about human nature. Most people will shift blame to something beyond their control. The reality is that the only good excuse is loss of a limb or consciousness. If you're still present and mobile, there is something you could have done to make your idea a reality. It may have required great sacrifice, but if you were breathing and not severely incapacitated, you could have made it happen.

Most people will not admit this. They'll give many reasons why something beyond their control made a difference but they will ignore their role. Your goal is to learn from this and also assume that everything that happens is your fault entirely. Even if it isn't, this primes your mind to learn from mistakes instead of shifting the blame. This way you can focus on improving the things you can control instead of blaming the things you can't.

Self-discipline and self-control will determine the quality of your life more than anything else.

It doesn't matter how intelligent you are or what connections you were born into. People born with so much money and influence that they never have to work are so rare that they aren't worth discussing. What is worth discussing is how you can achieve a lifestyle comparable to these lucky few.

Your ability to do what needs to be done when you don't want to do it will make all the difference in the world. The harder the task, the more valuable it tends to be. The more valuable, the more someone will pay you for doing it. It may take an investment of time, but it is worth more than a task that requires a minimal skill set.

Self-discipline allows you to develop the skills to improve your life. Self-control prevents you from making mistakes that will jeopardize your progress. If you get in trouble with the law, or have a kid you can't afford, or use your youth unwisely, then you will always be fighting an uphill battle in life.

Those are the big examples but the list is not exhaustive. Make sure you don't have to apologize to yourself in 10 years for some dumb shit you do today. Self-discipline to do the important things. Self-control to avoid the things that are going to ruin your life.

CHAPTER THREE
Standards

Your life will either be a great example or a horrible warning.

Everything you do will affect the people around you. They will see you as either someone worth aspiring to be or someone to avoid becoming. Regardless of how you influence people, you will have an effect. You must decide whether people should aim to be like you or differentiate themselves from you. Will people succeed because of you or will they triumph in spite of you? Use your life however you see fit, but remember: there is no neutrality. You will either be an inspiration or a cautionary tale.

Actionable Advice

Identify someone in your life to mentor. Ideally, the person is someone that you see on a semi-regularly basis but this isn't necessary. You can imagine that you are a role-model for children or other people struggling to deal with some issue.

Many adults look to other adults for guidance and inspiration. Your goal is to see your life through their eyes and decide if you're the type of person they want to become. Apply this to all aspects of your life, hopefully feeling the motivation to correct your inadequacies as you encounter them. Peer pressure works in both directions. You can elevate or degenerate based on what people expect of you. Use this knowledge to improve yourself.

It's easier to ask for forgiveness than permission? Fuck either of those. Do what must be done. You don't owe anyone an explanation.

If you worry what another person thinks, deep down you believe that you need their permission to succeed. This is, in effect, living for another person at the expense of your desires. This is a mistake. You can't live for other people.

Instead, you must always do what is best for you and your family. This way you don't need to worry about permission or forgiveness because your actions are always done with proper conviction. The opinions of others become irrelevant. You won't need to explain yourself because the results or your actions speak for themselves.

Actionable Advice

Take more action without approval or explanation. For example, if you have to end a phone call or leave someplace, merely excuse yourself and take off. Many people only feel comfortable giving a reason for doing something. Our goal is to develop the habit of doing the best thing for ourselves without the need for approval.

This isn't to be misinterpreted as an excuse to be rude. Good manners and standing up for yourself are not mutually exclusive. They only seem that way to people who want to take advantage of you. For example, when leaving a party you can say, "Thanks for having me." Your body language and tonality will go a long way in making it clear that your decision is beyond negotiation. This can be done with tact.

The biggest challenge you'll face is staying humble while your self-improvement pushes you past everyone.

It's natural to take pride in anything you do. The greater the effort required and the greater the difficulty of the task, the greater the pride resulting from accomplishing it. It's impossible to not feel pride when everyone can see that you have achieved a challenging milestone. It's difficult to stay humble in this scenario because a large part of humility is downplaying your achievements and diverting credit away from yourself. This is a clash of between natural tendency and what is socially acceptable. It's easy to forget that you are where you want to be today because of the hard work that you have already done. Especially if others think otherwise.

When people complain about their situation and you've put the effort into improving your position in life, it's immensely frustrating. Aside from not understanding their complacency about things which they claim to be very important, you aren't able to relate to people who do not approach life the same way. You will view their effort to living life as inferior. If you are getting what you want from life through effort, then you'll have limited patience for those who won't work.

Actionable Advice

Do not hold people to the same standard that you hold yourself to. When tempted to feel frustration towards people who are lazy and complain about their situation in life, remember that life is structured like a mountain: the higher you go, the less space there is so there are fewer people you have to deal with. The people that made it this high are likely to have similar attitudes, work ethic, and aspirations. It's how they got so high up the mountain. You get to enjoy a better view, cleaner air, and better company. Continue to work hard and you will inhabit higher and higher spaces in life. The higher you go, the less complaining you have to endure.

Learn to handle a level of stress that would break most people.

The world is too hard for most people. To keep people from giving up or checking out, the level of competition in the world has fallen. When things get a little difficult, most people give up. The best things in life are found where the level of stress breaks most people. If you can learn to thrive here, then you will be a winner. This is guaranteed.

Actionable Advice

Learning to suffer is important because suffering never ends. You have trouble coping with the excruciating parts of life because you believe they exist as punishment or retribution. The reality is that pain is as much a part of life as happiness. When something hurts, remind yourself that this is a part of life. Learn to embrace it and you will get more out of life.

This idea is not as esoteric as it may seem. For example, when I am running and it becomes unpleasant, I focus on the unpleasantness of the run. Rather than distract myself from the pain, I refocus on it and use it as a rallying point. I recognize that this is as much a part of my run as the good feelings that come upon completion. When we experience psychological or emotional pain, we must remember that the pain is part of life. Wishing it away doesn't help. Distracting ourselves from it doesn't help. Embrace it to enhance your focus and resolve for dealing with the problem at hand.

The problem with excuses isn't in giving them to other people. It's that you actually start believing that shit is what's holding you back.

Self-talk is incredibly powerful. Because you are the person that you listen to the most, the language you use is very important. Every word you think to yourself will morph you into a particular type of person. This may not be the person you want to be, but it is the person you have talked yourself into becoming. For better or worse, whatever you tell yourself will become your personal reality. How you see the world is what creates your experience because the only thing you control in this world is how you experience it.

Actionable Advice

Speak to yourself like a winner and you will act like a winner. Speak to yourself like a loser and you will act like a loser. When you make excuses, you run the risk of your brain actually believing the circumstances of the story you tell yourself. An excuse is just like any other piece of self-talk. You risk taking on the persona of one that perpetually makes excuses. That person is not the kind of individual that you want to become. Develop greater awareness of the words you use to communicate with yourself.

When someone breaks the rules you set for yourself, you get a choice: extinguish the relationship or live with not being true to yourself.

Whatever you allow in your life will persist, whether you want it to or not. This is because attitudes and behaviors take the path of least resistance. If something or someone with an undesirable disposition stumbles upon a path of low resistance, then they will remain there as long that path offers little opposition. If you are disrespected, you have 3 options.

First, leave the situation and cease all interactions. This is preferable if you have the ability to do this, but sometimes you can't. Second, stand up to the individual and correct them. Regardless of the outcome, you reinforce the attitude that people will not mistreat you. This causes you to carry yourself in a way that makes it less likely that the next person will try to treat you like a pushover.

The third option is the worst. You allow the disrespect and do nothing. In this instance, you reinforce the attitude that people can mistreat you. You start to carry yourself like a person that permits themselves to be disrespected and mistreated. Because of your demeanor, it is more likely that the next person will push you over.

Never believe you are less. Never let yourself get treated as if you are less. Force people to treat you with respect, and you forge the identity of a winner. Let people walk all over you, and you forge the identity of a doormat.

Actionable Advice

Treat all people with respect. Treat each human being you meet with the default respect you'd give to your parents. If you approach each situation like this, you're more likely to elicit respect in return. You'll also have more respect for yourself. This is a natural transition when you make a habit of treating others with respect.

Never tolerate disrespect. The mind is so powerful it might convince you that you deserve it since you did nothing to stop it.

Respect is not a guarantee. It is something that you must earn, but the effort put forth to earn it is the real prize. Disrespect is not a guarantee either. It is something that happens when you let your surroundings degrade to the lowest level. The disarray of your life is the real penalty.

The best way to increase the amount of respect you receive in your life is to do things that make you worthy of respect. This works for increasing the disrespect you experience as well. Nature abhors a vacuum. If you're not acting in a way that makes people respect you, then you're behaving in a way that invites disrespect. You're either progressing or regressing. You either stop disrespect by becoming someone to respect or you encourage disrespect by becoming someone worthy of the treatment.

Actionable Advice

When in doubt about the best way to act, ask yourself if you'd be proud of your children or parents acting this way. We want the best for those around us, and part of the best means being treated as someone worthy of respect. If you don't think a behavior would cause someone you care about to be viewed in high esteem and treated with respect, then you reconsider it. Choose the respectful line of action instead.

If you have high standards for your life, you automatically inoculate yourself against detrimental and wasteful relationships.

Low-quality individuals don't only have bad habits for themselves, but also in how they treat people. This the first danger of associating with no desire to become better. They are more likely to treat you like someone that doesn't want better either.

Because they lack respect for their own well-being, they engage in habits and mindsets that continually drag them lower. This is why many of their actions are the things a person with nothing to lose would do. While this may be true for them, it can't be true for you. Especially if you are reading this book.

Actionable Advice

The best way to protect yourself from these types of people is to stay away from them. That is obvious. However, many times they are drawn to you. For some people, it's as simple as telling them to go away. For the non-heartless amongst us a better method is to have a standard so high for your life that you repel them.

Once you accept that you're different from others and refuse to make apologies for it, your peace will increase exponentially.

There is no happiness found in trying to fit in. This is because it forces upon you a highly unnatural state of existence. The further you are from the average, the more energy it will take to force you to become part of them. At some point, it takes less energy to move further out than it does to be closer. This is the great secret that escapes many people. One of the great barriers to building a happy life is looking for it in the wrong direction.

For some people, this means moving closer to the average. These people not exceptional and trying to be would take more energy than it's worth. They are close to the middle of the curve where everyone is clustered. To move to the ends of the curve isn't worth it. The same idea is true for people that exist at the tails. It costs too much energy to move back to the middle.

It's challenging if you're half way there. It's the same distance in either direction, so how do you decide what is the best way to go for a life of happiness? Let's revisit a basic idea about happiness: Happiness is not a destination, but a journey. The more challenging the journey, the happier we are when we complete it. Therefore, we should move in the direction that presents a greater challenge. Now it would not make sense to do this if the completing the journey was beyond your ability. However, I believe that you are half way there, you can go further.

Embrace all of the things that make you unique. Live a

life that pushes you to the best of your ability. Your life will be unfulfilling and unhappy if you live under the weight of conformity. The way to escape this burden is to differentiate yourself as much as possible. This is accomplished by doing different and challenging things. Completion of each task brings you peace of mind and affirms that you are truly a unique entity, suitable to stand out.

Givers need to set limits because takers rarely do.

Many people are like vampires except they don't feast on blood. Instead, they suck you dry of your money, time and energy. The only reason a homeless man doesn't ask for all of your money is because he understands that there is a very reasonable limit to most people's generosity. Many forms of abuse take the form of vampirism.

If you do not set a limit on what people can get from you, you will find yourself worn down as they selfishly take from you. They have little regard for your well-being because you are just sustenance to them. If you, the giver, does not set a limit, then the taker will take everything.

Actionable Advice

The most powerful word in the English language is the word "no". You don't need to explain why you can't do something. If you can become comfortable telling people no when you can't or won't do something, then you greatly increase your personal power. You'll appear rude only to people that want to take advantage of you. Those with good intentions will not feel slighted by your opposition. Practice saying the word no without an excuse. As usual, this is not an excuse to be rude but it is imperative that you get used to declining an offer or request without feeling bad.

If you don't aim too high, then you're aiming too low.

Always aim farther than the goal. Extra effort acts as insurance against failure. Even if you fall short, you'll fall short of a position that is ahead of the goal. If you aim to just reach your goal, then falling short means falling short behind the goal. This is why they tell sprinters to run through the line and boxers to punch through the target. Approach each goal with the intention of exerting more effort than it seems you need.

Your reserves will run low, you'll encounter a setback, and you'll need to dig deep to accomplish what you want. Unpredictable but inevitable setbacks and detours will drain your energy. If you only have enough energy to cross the finish line, then you will not have anything left after you deal with the unexpected. When filled with excess, you have more to give and so the inevitable, unpredictable setbacks will not cost you victory.

Actionable Advice

There is a great book by Grant Cardone called "The 10X Rule." The basic idea is that however much energy you think it will take to do something, you need to put forth 10 times that to achieve results for certain. Not only does it guarantee success, it greatly reduces the amount of time it will take to reach your goals. To experience the power of this idea, pick a tiny goal that you would normally give yourself a 30-day time period to accomplish.

For example, let's say your goal is to write a short story. This is easily do-able in a 30-day period. But now your goal is to do it in 15 days. The particular goal isn't important for this piece of action. All that matters is that it's something you're fairly confident you could accomplish in 30 days.

As you raise your value more people will want more of you while you want less of them.

There is a funny thing about the way people interact. The more value a person has, the more people want to be around that person. However, the mere act of raising value means that you will not have the time or energy for most people. This means that valuable people are less interested in spending time with the masses of people than most. So here we have a situation where the greater a person's value, the more people want to spend time with them; however, they are less interested in spending time with people.

This explains why people of a similar level of achievement and status often pair up platonically and romantically. People simply don't understand what life is like at different levels. This lack of understanding is responsible for many of the conflicts that people experience when they suddenly improve their life past the average of their friend group.

The group can't understand the changes and perceives them as negative. The one raising his value can't understand the negativity and erroneously attributes it to jealousy or "hate", when in reality it is simply a misunderstanding and mismatch. The changing of position disrupts all players in the game, even those who are on the same side.

Actionable Advice

Most people are too concerned with their own problems to waste energy wishing for bad things to happen to you. Unless you have actively wronged a person, any ill will you experience towards you about your success is because shifting positions makes people uncomfortable. The human being will react first with fear before support. Most times it isn't hate towards you. It's fear that your improvement confirms their worst insecurities about themselves. Carry this with you in your heart and mind. Examine your own attitudes towards successful people.

The higher your standards for the people that get your time the happier you are. This is either painfully obvious or completely mind blowing.

You have a finite amount of time on this planet. You must set standards for who gets a piece of your precious time. It is not for me or anyone else to say exactly what the standard should be, but without any everyone will have access to your time and energy. This means that there will be many wasteful outlets for your energy to escape.

Because there is no filter, the people that drain your resources will be of a lower quality. This is a recipe for unhappiness. If you let everyone have part of your time, then there is nothing special or important about it (by definition). You won't have time to nurture bonds already present in your important relationships. Standards are the only way that people know they are special. Your time is the most valuable thing you can give to a person because it is finite.

You must be selective with your time otherwise, it's meaningless. Since relationships with people are the most important thing for your happiness, it is vital that you maintain them. Selectivity with your time so that you save it for building relationships is important for this reason.

Actionable Advice:

To be selective with your time and energy, it is important to know who the most important people in your life are. The following exercise will seem trite for some, but for others, it will be remarkably revealing.

List the 5 people you want to be in the room with you when you die. It is irrelevant why you want them there.

Do you want your parents, your children, your lover, your good friends, or maybe it's none of these people? The answer might surprise you, but do not analyze or judge. Merely use this as a tool for discovering which relationships you cherish. If you do not like the answer, then further digging is required into why you value those relationships or why you don't value the ones you feel you should.

Once you internalize that the world will go on no matter how you feel, you never look for pity again.

Feelings are part of being human. With notable exceptions (sociopaths), it's impossible for a person to cease having an emotional reaction. You can change your perspective but if something causes an emotional reaction in you, this is not unnatural. However natural this is, it doesn't mean that the world will care. Other human beings are concerned with their own feelings and the laws of the universe continue to work a certain way no matter what.

Once you understand that your emotions don't have the power to change the world, then you stop focusing so much on how you feel. This doesn't stop you from having an emotional response to the world. It does, however, make sure that you don't let your emotional state keep you from doing what needs to be done. People that let their hurt feelings prevent them from doing what's necessary usually end up with more hurt feelings.

Actionable Advice

Go one full day without using the statement "I feel...". If your position or idea cannot be expressed in terms of reason and logic, then it is not valid and you should not speak it. This is the speech portion of this idea but it can go deeper. If you find that it is easy to eliminate this phrase for your lexicon, you are no longer permitted to discuss how something makes you feel.

You can lend an ear to the emotional expressions of others and be supportive, but at no time are you ever allowed to mention how something makes you feel. Try to make it through one day doing this. Then another. Ultimately it will become natural to no longer focus on your feelings and instead on your effect in the world.

Getting rid of people who disrespect you is the only way you learn to respect yourself. Family, friends, lovers, whatever. They gotta go.

The easiest way to increase your self-respect is to improve the caliber of people around you. Higher quality people are more likely to treat you better and thus increase your self-respect. It's easier to feel like you're worth something when everyone around you treats you like you're worth something.

The corollary to this is that you must avoid people that disrespect you. There is no benefit to being around those who disrespect you and plenty to gain by distancing yourself from them. Why would you want to spend time around those who don't respect you anyway? Even if you succeed, it will be in spite of—not because of—your environment. You want the greatest chance of success and happiness and that means creating an environment that brings out the best in you.

Actionable Advice

If you have a problem building a circle of people that respect you, the best place to start is by learning to respect yourself. This means learning to spend time with yourself, away from a distracting or degrading environment.

You are to spend an hour a day alone working on something that makes you respect yourself. It is during this time that you gain confidence in your worth. This self-confidence works as a repellent against those that would disrespect you and a magnet for those of a high caliber. Continuing with this practice will have other benefits on your psyche and confidence as well.

Make people step their game up to deal with you. You're better off going at it solo otherwise.

You can only go as far as your greatest liability. You can only move as fast as the slowest person you deal with. Many people enjoy the feeling of being the best person in the group—the big fish in the small pond—but this is a great limitation. The problem with the big fish in a small pond is that the pond limits his growth. You have to leave your comfort zone to improve your life.

A strong move to improve your life is to cut off people that can't keep up with you. It need not be malicious or blatant, but if you're making the right moves then many people won't be able to keep your pace anyway. Some people feel bad about this and they let it hold them back. If you stifle your potential so that you can remain comfortable, this is a failure. If you embrace becoming the version of yourself and leave everything else behind, then you have a chance at greatness.

Actionable Advice

The best way to get people to move at your speed is to accomplish a few things alone. This will make people see the value you bring and the seriousness of your purpose. It will attract people who want to move with life changing speed and efficiency. It will repel those who don't. Your goal then is to make notable solo accomplishments towards your goal without any assistance.

Even if your ultimate dream isn't possible without the help of others, you have to prove to yourself and others that you are worthy of building a strong and capable team. The best way to do this is to become a strong and capable leader. This means accomplishing things first and seeking greater support later.

The only good excuse is death.

The difference between an excuse and a reason is intent. If you don't intend to accomplish something, you can easily find an excuse. When you are committed to a course of action, you begrudgingly accept a reason it did not happen. This is only after you've exhausted all of the options for success.

The difference between a good reason and a good excuse is whether you could make this happen if your life was on the line. If the answer is yes, then you have an excuse. It may be a good excuse. It may even be—give the circumstances—a reasonable excuse. But if you wanted the outcome badly enough, then the only thing that would stop you is death or the imminent threat of it.

Actionable Advice

Think about the things you wanted to happen in your life but they did not come to fruition. Make a list of all the reasons they did not occur. List any reason that comes to mind. When you have finished, look at the reasons and separate them into two categories: things are dependent on your actions and things that are a result of environmental factors beyond your control. For the things that are outside your control, deeply reconsider how it was actually within your power to avoid.

Even if there was an obvious outside cause, for the purposes of this exercise, only consider the ways in which you are responsible. Even if it means you should have looked both ways 3 more times before crossing the street so you wouldn't have gotten hit by the drunk driver, that's what it takes. This is the level of scrutiny you must approach your life so that you may see where you can avoid making excuses. The point of this exercise is to train you for maximum responsibility.

Dudes can be basic too. Just drink shitty beer, know all the sports stats, never approach a girl sober and watch every show on Netflix.

If you want to lead an average life, follow the suggestions of the masses on how to spend your "free" time. Men are encouraged to become sports junkies, drink cheap beer at happy hour and binge watch new shows on some streaming video service. This is not so much the path to mediocrity as it is the blueprint for building a woefully average existence. Your entire life is becomes centered around consuming instead of producing anything interesting.

Basic dudes are called basic because their daily lives aren't much better than the lowest level of existence. There is nothing challenging or growth inducing about their lifestyle. They are merely coasting along. Because so much of the population is at or below average, this culture is often celebrated. The "Dad Bod" is becoming popular as a symbol of the modern male. The basic male is a stereotype of consumption and a caricature of wayward masculinity.

Actionable Advice:

The irony is that to avoid the fate of a basic male, you must do things that most males should (and used to) do. Take up weight lifting or a combat sport. The aggression and training of your body will increase your testosterone and make you more eager to engage in life.

Most importantly, it will make you disgusted with all of the ways that men let themselves deteriorate into consumption junkies. Even working on your body is a type of production. This is the easiest place to start and where you will see the biggest results. Therefore, it is the first place to start to reverse the possibility of becoming a basic dude.

The hard part is the gap where you've left the old you behind but aren't secure with the new you. Don't regress. It is darkest just before dawn.

The unsexy side of self-improvement is the part where you are improving. As you leave behind what was once comfortable and familiar, you enter the realm of the unknown. Mistakes will be made that appear to set you back and leave you worse than when you started. Do not despair, for this is a sign of progress. Most people never try to improve because they do not like the feeling of incompetence that accompanies the trial and error they must endure. However, this is a necessary proving ground you must train in.

The gap between the old and new is where you struggle most to become the best version of yourself. If you are able to persist in the dark and learn how everything works, then you eventually earn the ability to live in the light. It's a treacherous journey, but each successful step gets you closer to the light. Even when you hit an obstacle, it hurts temporarily but the pain subsides. You are left with the knowledge of what to avoid on your path towards the light.

Actionable Advice

Remember this: Most people are uncomfortable with moving in the dark. Of those that decide to move in the dark, many are uncomfortable with the pain of learning where the obstacles are and making mistakes. They will give up and retreat to the corner of the room before the darkness. Only the brave souls continue moving forward until they are basked in the light. Light is the reward for risk, darkness is the punishment of playing it safe.

Not Caring What Other People Think Is A Super Power

As you improve, your tolerance for excuses decreases. As does your tolerance for mediocrity. Few people are worth your time at that point.

As you improve your life, you won't be able to understand why others won't do the same. Once you experience the power of action over complaints, you will no longer be able to tolerate people that refuse to improve. This is a natural and expected consequence. You begin to see how the mentality of settling creeps into every facet of a person's life. It will disturb you.

Your first instinct will be to convince people to take a path out of the rut. We all do this and it's natural. But after the discussions result in arguments and disagreement (they always do) you learn that it's pointless. The best you can do is let them be, but also realize that you don't fit in. Once you wake up to the world around you, you can never go back to sleep. To find your place of comfort you must abandon what you once knew.

When you live true to yourself, you look forward to rejection.

The better you know yourself and what is important to you, the less energy you need to resist attempts to influence your thinking. The problem is that most of the world is trying to influence you to think or act or a certain way. As you become more sure about what you want from this life, you also realize how much of a distraction and waste of time anything else is.

You can only do so much to reject demands on your attention. However, sometimes the world will deem your perspective or approach to be unacceptable. Though at first this may seem problematic, but it is actually great. Rejection is the best thing that can happen to you because it automatically filters out potential time and energy wasters. This is because being a good fit works both ways.

You can decide which relationships or opportunities are wasteful and which are worthwhile. The way to do this is an unyielding commitment to your vision. This will polarize everything, increasing your rate of rejection and automatically saving you time. It also attracts better fits for your life. There is no loss in this situation. When you live aligned with what is important, you welcome rejection

CHAPTER FOUR

Time, Confidence and Sobriety

Risk taking is essential to any endeavor.

The greater the reward, the more work it requires. The nature of hard work is that the outcome is not a guarantee. The only thing hard work does is increase your odds of success. Because you are dealing with probabilities, sometimes you don't have the success you were planning for. Even if things are significantly stacked in your favor.

As you work to get the things you want out of life, remember this: One trait necessary for great success is risk tolerance. You must be comfortable knowing that you may never get exactly what you want. Most people need security so society is built to provide it. Once you decide you want more than the average person, you have to take a risk.

The further from the average you want to be, the more work it will take and the greater the possibility is that you won't succeed. While prudence is important, those seeking greatness do not concern themselves with the downside. They understanding risk taking is essential for any endeavor.

True confidence is when you do not fear outcomes.

It is impossible to guarantee a specific outcome. You can influence many things about an outcome but the final result is beyond your control. This is why placing your confidence in the outcome of an event always leads to anxiety and disappointment.

Consider a boxing match. You can't control what your opponent is doing. You can't control the conditions of the meeting. You can't control whether today will be the day you get injured or worse. So what can you control? Where can you afford to put your confidence?

You trust in the process. All the things mentioned above in your control do not concern whether you win or lose. They do not decide the outcome. They are processes that are under your control.

You can control your training, mindset, and conditioning. You can control your understanding of the strategies and tactics that will give you an edge.

By placing your confidence in the process that you control, you cease worrying about the outcomes that are a result. True confidence can develop because it is rooted in things that you control. You have control over your own mind, body, and spirit and its preparation. Only when you trust in that preparation and process can you truly be confident.

Never was anything great achieved without danger.

Danger represents a threat. The threat can be of any nature. All that matters is that that something of value is facing the possibility of harm. For great things to be accomplished, you must put your security and well-being on the line. It all comes back to the idea of distancing yourself from the average.

The further from average you are, the less of a safety net there is for you to fall on if things don't go well. This is because the world is designed for the average person. Great things are not for the average person.

To be great is to, by definition, be a risk taker. You can't have it any other way. The secure route is always waiting for you, but you know what's down that path. There is no risk, but there is nothing worth taking a risk for either. To experience danger in the face of well-calculated risk is the surest indicator that you are on the path to greatness.

Actionable Advice:

Do something not in your comfort zone and potentially embarrassing. The idea is to do something that has great pay-off potential in some aspect of your life.

When you stop drinking, your quantity of social interactions decreases but the quality of them increases.

Alcohol is a substance that lowers inhibitions. This means that it makes your social interactions flow more smoothly. The main reason for this is that you don't critique much of what you say. This is neither good or bad; it is merely a feature of alcohol. Some people have trouble socializing because they worry about how they'll be perceived, so it is used to decrease that worry.

Alcohol silences this inner critic. It lowers the dam that holds back our words and socialization. Sometimes the dam is lowered too far and behavior that should be conserved isn't. This is the risk we take when we rely on bottled shortcuts to do the hard work of modifying our personality.

When you cease making alcohol the focus of your social interactions, you no longer have this behavior modification shortcut. With your behavior conserved, each interaction requires greater energy and focus to proceed. Many of your friends and acquaintances will evaporate because their connection with you was not based on your authentic personality. However, the relationships that remain intact will be genuine because the connection is based on unmodified behavior.

Social energy is finite. The energy that was spread thinly across many social interactions gets concentrated into a few. With more energy for fewer social interactions, the quality of the interactions dramatically improves. Because the interactions are improved, you won't need to have as many of them. It is the difference between eating a lot of terrible meals versus a few high-quality meal.

Don't procrastinate by wasting the time you have left before you die.

Procrastination is a challenge to overcome. I will not pretend that I have the answer or that I am immune to the charms of putting off till tomorrow what can be done today. Instead, I offer a different way to look at procrastination. If you digest this, you'll feel uneasy when deciding to not do something. Associating procrastination with discomfort is the first step in overcoming it.

Procrastination neglects mortality. You will die one day and each thing you don't do is one less thing you ever can do. Even routine tasks, if put off until later, force you to compress more things into a finite amount of time. The time you have left in the world isn't usually known, but we do know that it is a fixed amount. This means that you never get that time back. You have wasted a finite supply of a non-renewable resource.

Almost no one knows their last day, and the ones that do are the exception for reasons they'd give anything to change. Your goal should be to enjoy as much of the time you have alive. Procrastination is a cruel thief that robs you of your most precious resource. Because you wait to do something that must be done anyway, you're reducing your overall available amount of time and generating unpleasant feelings. Doing another urgent task is not the same as procrastination. If you have multiple obligations, prioritizing them is not procrastination. Putting them off for less pressing matters is.

Disrespect of time is a great sin because it arrogantly

assumes that you will live forever. You have such little time to do things that it's a small miracle you accomplish anything at all. When you feel the desire to procrastinate, remember that you will die and each wasted moment is one that will never return. Write down three things you have to do today. Now get up and do them.

One of the best parts about not drinking is that people can't waste my time 'meeting up for drinks.

A tremendous amount of time is wasted under the pretense of "getting drinks." There is nothing wrong with drinking and it's fine to drink with friends, but alcohol decreases the quality of any interaction. Because the quality is decreased, you feel like you need to increase the quantity of them. This means you'll waste time with many people that you might not actually enjoy if alcohol wasn't the focal point.

When a person stops drinking, they have to make a whole new group of friends. This usually occurs because a person realizes three things when they aren't drinking:

1) Drunk people are obnoxious and annoying
2) Almost all of the typical drinking activities are centered around immobility
3) They don't actually like most of the people they drink with.

No one's behavior improves after the third drink. Despite claims to the contrary, you are not cooler or more interesting while drunk. You become a liability. Most of what you do while drinking is a sedentary activity like watching a sporting event or talking to people you wouldn't normally talk with sober. This is tolerable while drinking because it's part of the lifestyle, but once you stop drinking you realize that you can make better use of your time.

Remember: a lot of people are one missed happy hour away from loneliness. To these people, drinking with people they don't care for is better than drinking alone. They will drain your time and energy so they can feel better. When you don't drink, these people actively avoid you because you are like a stone to a vampire. There is no blood to suck so they have no interest in you.

There are few things better than a sober conversation with old friends.

If alcohol is not the center of your social gatherings, you quickly discover (or re-discover) one of the more enjoyable ways to increase the quality of the time spent with other people. Sober conversations are more fulfilling because they are conducted with a purpose as opposed to necessity. Meeting up for drinks with conversation is one thing; meeting up for a conversation with drinks is another.

People believe they are doing the latter, but most encounters are the former. The only way to be certain is to make it a point to experience the conversation without the drinks. A fully cognizant and aware conversation between two friends was once a common event but now it is terribly rare. Try reigniting this ritual with some close friends of yours.

Push the snooze button and you'll just end up working for someone who didn't.

Waking up early is special because it's a practice of discipline. I'm not referring to waking up early to get to class or work. If you have to do that, then this is your normal time to wake up. But if you can learn to wake up and spare yourself an extra 30 minutes to an hour, you learn that you are capable of doing quite a bit in this small window of time. An extra seven hours a week is enough to develop any skill set to the point where you can increase your value over the course of a year.

The people that make more than you used their time more wisely than you. As a result of using their time wisely, they end up with more time. Efficiency and early rising are two cornerstone habits of the productive and successful. The habits feed one another until they are able to do more than the average person with less time and because of that, they end up with more time.

If you want to be in an average position of having less of the things you want, then continue habits that take away from the time you have to improve. If you want to progress, work more efficiently. An extra hour a day quickly compounds if used correctly.

Actionable Advice

Unless you are at a place in life where you are content and accomplished, you won't suffer giving up an hour of sleep. You don't even need to sacrifice an entire hour. Thirty extra minutes a day devoted to a goal will add up over time. In one year, you will be closer to accomplishing your goal than if you had slept for 30 more minutes. You won't even be tired. Instead, you'll be energized to wake up each morning and work on what is most important to you.

But that is the key. You must have an important goal. It need not be important to the rest of the world but it must drive you to improve. If you don't have something in the world you want bad enough to force yourself to develop, then you will never do something as simple as waking up earlier. This is a tiny sacrifice. If you can not make it, you will never be able to make the real sacrifices that demand more of you.

Finding your purpose is good but sometimes you gotta get in touch with basic motivation. You want money, women and to prove people wrong.

The "Hierarchy of Needs" is a theory proposed by psychologist Abraham Maslow. The theory says that people have to satisfy one level of needs before moving on to another. The needs are shaped like a pyramid with self-actualization and creative outlets at the top, while our base requirements reside at the bottom. According to the theory, people don't focus on the top needs until they have the bottom fulfilled.

When you set out to motivate yourself into taking action, it helps to remember this pyramid. It's only a theory, but it's one where we can immediately see the implications in the real world. Very few people can write the next great novel if they are worried about how they're going to eat or where they're going to sleep. I'm sure it has happened, but we are always in the business of giving ourselves the best chance for success. Therefore, it makes sense that we seek money, attention, and recognition before anything else.

There is nothing wrong with doing a thing for the money or the fame. The danger lies in forgetting that it's only the base of the pyramid. You cannot live on a foundation alone. Your pyramid of motivation must go beyond the foundation because once you have satisfied your basic needs, you'll need a reason to keep going. Until then, you need a reason to start. Never feel bad for doing something just because you are motivated by material rewards.

ABR/
HIERA

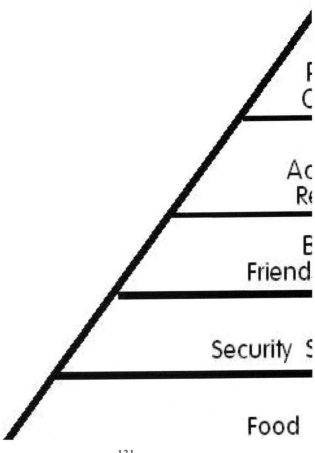

When improving you should be more scared of what will happen if you DON'T take action than.

You can be motivated in two ways: you can desire a thing in the future or you can fear returning to the past. Imagining a superior future can be difficult. There is also the complication of the present not being terribly difficult. You could have more and better with less frustration, but you've learned to settle. Getting motivated about a better future will be difficult for you. Instead, we pursue a different route for motivation.

Before we go further, you must remember a characteristic of the universe. Nothing in life is neutral. You are either pushing towards or moving away from something. You are either becoming better or worse. Imagine that you continue doing the same thing for the next 10 years that you've done for the last 10 years. Human actions and behavior is subject to inflation. The mere fact that you haven't improved over a decade means that you lost. If you aren't trying to get better, you're automatically getting worse.

Unless you have lived a significant portion of your life already, imagine doing the same thing 10 years from now. If it does not depress you, then you're either living a good life or a good delusion. Use the awful image of being in the same place doing the same things as motivation to be better.

If you remain motivated by external acquisitions, then you will never reach your true potential.

You must never fear being honest with yourself. If you are motivated by external rewards, then embrace this and use it to become the best version of yourself. However, you must be aware that these things are not going to sustain you. Especially once you attain them.

It is often said that the greatest saboteur of future success is past success. This is true if you are motivated by the trappings of success. If you're only doing the hard work to build a life of comfort, then what will make you sustain the work once you have acquired the lifestyle you desire?

While there is nothing wrong with initial external motivates, your motivations must switch to the internal. External motivation: women, fortune, and fame. Internal motivation: mastery, learning, pride. Start with the external. Mature to the internal. If you remain motivated by external acquisitions, then you will never reach your true potential.

CHAPTER FIVE

Poems

Illusion Keeper

The hardest part for the newly woke

Is letting sleeping dogs lie

The hardest part for the red pill taker

Is not to give up and cry

With awareness of the world and how it works, one becomes overwhelmed by two powerful feelings. The first feeling is soul-crushing cynicism. It's impossible for you to remain innocent and naive, for you are now aware of the true nature of people and the world. Your immense sadness will make you want to resign from the world. While you eventually learn to engage the world despite this, the melancholy eternally lingers in the background.

The second feeling is the urge to share your awareness of the world with others. This is a sensible response, for you care about the people around you and don't want them manipulated and mislead. Unfortunately, many people have no desire to wake up. They enjoy the lie and the comfort it brings. As Morpheus said in <u>The Matrix</u>, "The Matrix is a system. The very minds of the people we are trying to save. But until we do, these people are still a part of that system and that makes them our enemy. You have to understand, most of these people are not ready to be unplugged. And many of them are so inured, so hopelessly dependent on the system, that they will fight to protect it."

Actionable Advice

Find a way--even if it's small--to add positivity to the world. In this way, you combat the cynicism that comes with being "woke". When tempted to expose someone's naïve viewpoint, view them as a child and ask yourself, "If I told this kid that Santa Claus wasn't real, would they be happy or sad?" Most children need to believe in Santa Claus to make sense of the world they don't understand.

Illumination

What is the course when light alone

Won't drive the darkness out?

Whatever casts such sinister shadows

Must be destroyed now

An optimistic view is that the best way to combat something is to strike with its opposite. Love conquers hate, tolerance conquers bigotry, or even pleasure conquers pain. Because the typical reaction to the negatives is to meet them with more intense versions of the same negative, people who adopt this optimistic viewpoint see themselves as enlightened. They don't meet hate with more hate; they meet it with love. They don't meet violence with more violence; they meet it with peace. They don't curse the darkness; they light a candle.

The enlightened camp eventually faces a problem. There are some things that exist solely to destroy anything that does not agree with it. This is evil in the truest form. The problem with this evil is that it does not passively exist. It actively consumes and will devour all that you cherish if it isn't met with an appropriate force. There are evils that exist only to devour love, disrupt peace and demolish all you hold dear. It will slash the other cheek that you turn.

Actionable Advice

Turning the other cheek is often times the best response, but set a boundary. When that boundary is crossed, push back with a disproportionate force that sends the offender the clear message that you will not be helplessly devoured.

Wonderland

The rabbit hole may never end

And that's a scary thought

But neither do the lies you've been fed

So come and take a hop

Truth and falsehood cannot occupy the same space at the same time. A mind conditioned to look for the truth will never settle for lies. Sadly, the inverse of this is true as well. People do not like the truth because once you reveal one lie, you realize how many other lies were necessary to keep it standing. The weight of this structure is immense.

Eventually, you realize that it never ends so you have to make a choice: you can spend your life in a home built on a shaky foundation of lies or you can jump down the hole of truth. Lies are a comfortable home with a security system. Truth is a cold dark alley with bandits. From the comfort of your home, there is no potential to grow. From the alley, you can rise to the top of the city.

The price we pay for believing in falsehood is stifled growth. The gift to us for embracing truth is unlimited opportunity. Lies are attractive because they are easy to believe. Truth is repulsive because it makes you aware and awareness brings responsibility. To do something great with your life, you cannot embrace lies. Greatness comes from embracing responsibility. Responsibility comes from embracing truth. The rabbit hole of truth is scary, but you must take the hop.

Actionable Advice

There are things about yourself that are weak and inadequate. You may not fully admit your shortcomings to yourself, but you are intimately aware of them. Until you accept these shortcomings and admit to yourself that you are flawed, then you cannot do anything about them. Worse, your feelings about them are a weakness that can be used to manipulate you. With this piece of actionable advice, I seek to liberate you.

Make a private list of all the things about yourself that you are ashamed of. First just think of the things. This is the first step. Then get to point where you can write them down. Then look in the mirror and say them to yourself. You must hear your voice submit to admitting your inadequacies. Once you do this, tell yourself that you will improve them. You are not perfect, but there is no reason to settle. You are flawed like any other human but now you are attempting to remedy those flaws.

Raindrops

No matter how rough the day

Or how dreadful tomorrow seems

You're amongst the blessed

If the sound of raindrops

Carries you to rest

In every day there can be found something worth admiration. Likewise, every day contains an element of tragedy. The scale of it and your proximity to it don't matter as much as you think, for either you survive or you do not. This is a victory that may not be worthy of immense celebration, but temporarily closing your eyes at the end of the day is superior to closing them permanently at an undetermined time. This is something to be extremely grateful for and is worthy of admiration.

Actionable Advice

The gift of life is something we take for granted. Over 150,000 people die each day. This is a small percentage of the world's population, but it is still a very large amount. Therefore, not being part of the group of people that perish each day is a reason to be grateful. This means that no matter how bad the day was that came before, you have a chance to make the next day better. You have been given a blessing.

Style

That which is trendy

Will eventually fade

But that which has style

Forever will stay

The best way to stand out, make an impression and demonstrate that you have self-respect is to adopt a signature style. Style is not only your way of dressing but also your way of doing things. Likewise, styles and trends are not only limited to clothing.

Many people follow trendy diets to lose weight, trendy budgets to save money, popular methods of getting rich or even the hottest new language learning "hack" or method. In reality, the fundamentals and hard work are all that matter. Once you have those, you can tailor them to fit your particulars. Technical mastery comes before stylistic expression.

A style of doing things becomes a habit. The best path to a productive life is to live according to habits and lifestyles. When you abandon your style and habits in favor of a trendy temporary fix, you betray your habits. If you change how you dress in response to some trend, not only does it demonstrate a lack of confidence in yourself, it also demonstrates a lack of foundation.

Styles take time to develop. They take work. They take the risk, for there are no guarantees. It takes time to build comfort in your own style so if you constantly give in to trends, you will never invest the necessary time.

Actionable Advice

If you don't have a personal way of doing things, chances are it's because you continually give into external pressure and change. This is because you don't put up resistance to an overwhelming force. Lack of resistance is the result of a weak internal foundation and the overwhelming force comes from society telling you to change.

For the next 30 days, pick a small but noticeable and sustainable fashion statement. You can start wearing hats, a wrist watch, a certain style of shirt, etc. Whatever you decide to do, don't explain to anyone why you're doing it but graciously accept compliments. Do not respond to any criticisms. Getting comfortable with a stylistic decision leads to comfort in other decisions. This will lead to increased confidence in any habits and traits you develop to contribute to your overall style.

The Underachieved

Will without skill

Gets victory in a war of attrition

Skill without will

Results in unfulfilled ambition

You can work hard or you can work smart. People say this but most do not understand that the two are not mutually exclusive. Both are necessary for success. It is just as important to perform with maximum effort as it is to perform with maximum efficacy. The greater your skill, the less effort is needed to obtain the same result. The greater your effort, the more potent your execution.

If you neglect will power, you'll do fine until you encounter hard problems. If you neglect skill, you'll get blown out of the water by anyone with a modicum of discipline. When skill and will walk together, they abolish anything in their path. If you separate them, you're operating at half strength--at best. At worst, you lose all hope of accomplishing anything significant.

Actionable Advice

A straight line is the most efficient route between two points, but if you walk slowly then a sprinter on a curve will beat you. An efficient routine is essential to success, but so is working diligently along said routine. To experience this idea, create a short plan to clean your home.

Once you have that plan, try to do it as quickly as possible. The first time around you'll most likely discover that your original plan had some inefficiencies. Correct those inefficiencies, then continue with the same or increased level of effort. The way you come to think about this inconsequential problem can be extrapolated to solve more pressing issues in your life.

The Mutiny

Cruelty before kindness

Makes their loyalty strong

Kindness before cruelty

Soon your head will be gone

Good leaders understand that it's easier to relax the rules than tighten them up. This is why good parents are initially strict but let their child earn freedoms along the way. It takes more energy to organize chaos than it does to manage order. Therefore, when you're in charge of people, start with rigid structure and then--if you so please—loosen the reigns and have fun. Starting the other way is a recipe for trouble. Remember, it's a lot easier to let a trickle of water through a hose than it is to stop an unrestrained torrent.

Actionable Advice

Regardless of our position in life, we are all leaders of ourselves. All leadership starts with self-focus. Pick an area of your life that you are not satisfied with. This can be anything: your diet, appearance, spending habits, intelligence, etc. Create a plan to greatly improve it over the next 30 days.

The plan should be the most extreme and efficient way to your goal. For example: for diet, you go completely vegetarian or no-carb. For your spending habits, you ride your bike everywhere. For appearance, you're in the gym twice a day. For 30 days, you exist in a state of extreme toughness and dedication to your goal.

After 30 days, you can scale back a little. This is assuming you've made some progress. If you've dropped 10 pounds, then perhaps you introduce something back into your diet. You still will exercise restraint and control, but this gives you an opportunity to observe the effect of starting at the end of extreme control and gradually earning back your freedoms. This is a valuable feeling to experience if you are ever tasked with leadership.

The Shallows

Substance without style

Is the way of the nerd

Ignored and celibate

With his voice never heard

Human beings make judgments based on appearance and social acumen. You will be disappointed if you ignore this and believe that your skills, affluence or intelligence alone will make people like you. This is a hard realization for some people. Improving your appearance and social skills takes work, but not nearly as much as learning hard topics that only a select few have an interest in. If you can learn physics, then you have the aptitude to learn basic style and social skills.

If you feel like people should like you or want to date you just because you have affluence, skills or intelligence, dispose of that attitude. Remember: Those things are secondary. They make people curious about you and give you an audition, but no one will want to keep you around to work behind the scenes--let alone in a supporting or main role--if you don't look nice and carry yourself well.

Actionable Advice

Assume that every person you meet is the most shallow

human being the planet. Operate with the belief that they do not care about anything but how you look and how you make them feel. This is already true in most cases, but if you don't believe it then act on faith for a moment. To fortify your faith, remember that we pay more attention to better-looking people. There is a great deal of research which suggests better looking people have--all things considered equal—more success in life.

Perhaps you think your look is just fine. Maybe you're aware it could be better. If you're part of the latter, start with small changes and gradually work your way up. Many people don't realize that there is some anxiety that comes with the new found attention of being attractive. Read fashion blogs, start out making small adjustments and notice the reception you get from people.

The Fundamentals

Speed is overrated

Fundamentals are overlooked

Patience is no longer a virtue

For these reasons, you'll never be good

In any endeavor, one must always aim towards control and patience. Speed is a wonderful attribute, but it takes a lot of energy and it's difficult to control. A warrior needs patience, timing and wisdom to discern vulnerabilities and the best course to attack to them. These things take time to develop and aren't as sexy as speed, but you won't need to be faster when you understand the correct thing to do every time.

Neo: What are you trying to tell me? That I can dodge

bullets?

Morpheus: No, Neo. I'm trying to tell you that when

you're ready, you won't have to.

(The Matrix)

Actionable Advice

Seek deep understanding of why you do a certain thing. When you have that understanding, you won't need to rely on any gimmick to achieve success. The physical equivalent of this is speed, but it reminds me of something a physics professor once told me. He warned that I should not use a formula unless I can derive it.

In other words, once I understand a concept so well that I can create the formula from it, then I can use the formula to save time. The kicker is at this level of understanding I wouldn't need to use the formula anyway. Deep understanding of your craft ensures that you have the solution faster than if you rely on speed and shortcuts to solve your problem.

Kaizen

Some years might be marginal

Some years might be great

But each year should be better

With small improvements each day

Even if only by a marginal stroke

May you go to sleep better

Than how you awoke

Progress never happens as fast as we like. At times it moves at a crawl. At times we feel like we're going nowhere. The worst are the times it feels like we are regressing. In these moments we must not despair. As long as we are practicing and learning--even if we lack flawless execution--there is progress. Our mind is sorting the new task out even if we aren't consciously working on it. Over time, it adds up and the result is a great output. Sometimes the output comes immediately after new things are added. Sometimes it takes a year. As long as we are putting in new things, our brain is working to do something great.

Actionable Advice

Accept that there are no shortcuts to becoming exceptional. With this you must also accept that the path to greatness is not linear. Because of these two factors, understand that progress is merely the flower that grows from the deep roots of time and effort. Focus on the learning and competence. Mastery and success are the inevitable results.

Feminine Charm

The strongest amongst us

Can be made weak

By that which is pretty

Slender and sweet

Women are simultaneously the greatest weakness and motivator of men. The same face that can inspire you to kill a man in their defense can make you break down in tears. It can make you feel loved and inspired or forsaken and cursed. No matter how powerful a heterosexual man is, there will always be a woman that is his Helen of Troy.

Actionable Advice

If you're a man, be aware of the power that a woman has over you simply by being a woman. This is why advertisements for vices--things that we logically know we should not put in our body--have women in them. If you're a woman, be cognizant of the power that your beauty and feminine nature bestow upon you. Knowing how a thing works is half the battle.

Stoic

Even if you ventured

And nothing was gained

Still your tongue

And never complain.

If you want to remain sane

Change the world or it stays the same

That in life which makes you cry

Cannot be handled if you never try

Don't complain. Even if there is something worth complaining about. Especially if there is something worth complaining about. Complaining is motivated by an inability to take responsibility. This is a core trait of complainers. If complaining is a symptom, irresponsibility is the virus. Once infected, the host is likely to blame everyone and everything for their problems. Except themselves. A pessimistic attitude and victim complex are soon to follow.

All complaints send the same message: I want this situation to be better, but I don't want to fix it myself.

Now, like a young child whose life also lacks responsibility, the complainer's life is full of wishes. These are wishes for a better future instead of a plan for improvement that involves work. It does no good to complain. The world only improves through action.

Actionable Advice

If you're ever in a mood to complain, remember this quote, "Be kind and lower your eyes, for everyone is fighting a harder battle." This has been etched in my mind and heart for years. This idea acts as a powerful antidote to the complaining virus. By keeping you humble in the face of other's struggles, it forces you to take the focus off of yourself. It also reminds you that not only can things get worse; they actually are for some people.

The universe has not picked you out for specific torture. The nature of universal suffering is impersonal. From now on, lower your eyes and refuse to complain about anything. This is the way of the capable through strength, humility, and empathy.

Inconvenient Truth

The world looks to a thinking man

Peculiar and so strange

That which should be obvious

Is met with great disdain

The problem with thinking is that so few people actually do it. When you take the time to formulate a responsible response to a problem, you quickly realize that this is a rare action. Most people have formed their opinions based on knee-jerk emotional responses and prejudice. Much of the insanity in our world is the result of people feeling that something is wrong and then using emotion, rather than reason, to remedy the situation.

Difference of opinion is fine and expected, but many people do not have a solid base of empirical thought for their feelings. This causes them to experience great turbulence when confronted with reality. Reality does not care about your feelings. Only what is true. When you live according to your feelings, you meet reality with great disdain.

Actionable Advice

Charlie Munger once said, "I'm not entitled to have an opinion unless I can state the arguments against my position better than the people who are in opposition. I think that I am qualified to speak only when I've reached that state." The beauty of this statement is that it ensures that whatever opinion you have, you at least will have thought deeply about it.

Though everyone is entitled to an opinion, that doesn't mean they're all sensible or valid. Thinking deeply about one's position reveals which of your thoughts are controversial and which are merely ridiculous.

Silent Sensibility

Be careful when you speak the truth

It often is misheard

What sounds like common sense to you

To others seems absurd

Attempts to change human nature will always be met with failure. This is because the human being is the way it is, it always has been that way, and it will always be that way. The best we can do is punish the severe disruptions to our way of life, mitigate the less severe, and ignore most everything else.

It's absurd to believe that you can change the basis of human behavior. You can only influence it through subtle manipulations and overt incentives. People who think otherwise have an ideal--not based on truth or reality--so when you confront them with truth and reality, it sounds absurd to them.

Actionable Advice

The greatest benefit of this information is that it teaches the value of silence. You cannot reason with a mob. A mob is fueled by emotions and righteousness. Either you're with them or against them. Though people are different in the things they're irrational about, collectively this irrational mindset is like a mob.

Your thorough analysis of a situation will not be appreciated. It will make you the outcast of a group. If you are not interested in making a change or need to feel like you belong, still your tongue when encountered by an irrational mob. Do not attempt to change their mind. Your words will be viewed as those of an insane man and you will be treated accordingly.

The Courageous

A strong heart with a weak mind

Gets taken advantage of many times

A strong mind with a weak heart

Makes one craft plans they never start

With every important decision, you must weigh two factors which are often--but not always--at odds with one another. How you think about something and how you feel about it. Acting based on how you feel is done to avoid pain, though ironically it often leads to exactly that. Acting purely on rational thought will often alienate others and cause you to lose parts of your humanity.

All the analysis in the world does not make one passionate to engage in life; even if it's calculated to be a good idea. Likewise, no matter how bad you feel for someone or a situation, you must do what is best. Even if it feels the worst. Never forget that the road to hell is paved with good intentions.

Actionable Advice

Good judgment is balanced judgment. The balance is between mercy and justice. Absolute justice leads to a society gripped by fear while absolute mercy leads to anarchy. You must be hard on yourself and forgiving of the world. Balance is struck in the following manner: unforgiving justice on ourselves and our standards but unlimited mercy for the world.

Lemmings

Groupthink makes people

Do the craziest shit

That if they were alone

They'd never commit

You are the average of the 5 people you spend the most time around. Almost everyone is aware of that. What people neglect is how powerful that information really is. I don't know if there is a proper word for this phenomena, but at times people act like lemmings. All it takes is a few people doing the same thing and suddenly everyone else thinks it's a good idea. They think to themselves, "well they're acting in unison. I better do the same thing too!".

I'm sure there is a more scientific explanation than that, but I have to believe that mob mentality makes reasonable people shed sound judgment because the larger group has abandoned sensibility. The "5 people" rule is just the tip of the iceberg. It's important to carefully select the environment you spend the most time in as well as the caliber of people you spend the most time with--even if only in a casual sense.

Actionable Advice

If you're improving your life, you are better off alone

than surrounded by people who don't share your ambition. You will either end up ostracized from the group or assimilated back into their way of thinking. This is a challenge that many people face when striving towards a better life. They want friends and a social circle but if your friends aren't lifting you up then they're dragging you down. Nothing in life is neutral and that includes your relationships. The behavior isn't intentional but the effect is very real. This means that you'll have to make a choice.

If you care more about being liked and belonging, continue spending time around the people who don't have the same goals as you. They'll probably leave you alone, but their lifestyle and habits will directly clash with yours. If you want to be successful, cut them all off and focus on your new life and the new habits that come with it. You will eventually meet new people that you have more in common with. This group will be more conducive to your future plans. Here you will find unwavering support.

Intent

Words are often meaningless

While actions deceive and hide

Intent is the only thing to read

To catch what's between the lines

People have evolved to lie very well. However, nature does not enjoy a great imbalance. Every predator eventually become prey. Even human beings are now encountering bacteria and viruses that are resistant to the best drugs. They will most certainly kill many people and thus balance will be restored. So with good liars, nature has evolved more complex ways to catch them.

The most useful tool in discerning if someone is lying is learning to read intent. Words can mean anything so they mean nothing. Actions only reveal what has been done. Intent is true because it is difficult to disguise. When a person is reading faces, the micro-expressions reveal intent. The micro-expressions come quickly before a person has time to disguise their true intent with crafted words. If you can read intent, then you are reading minds.

Actionable Advice

To become a better lie detector, you must pay attention

to people. You need to build a mental database of facial expressions and what they mean. The only way to do this is to interact with many people. There is a game I used to play when I was improving my ability to read intent.

First, you need to grab a book on reading body language. Have a quick read through, make some notes, and then go to a place where people meet and talk. I used to go to a bar. That's as good of a place as any.

Observe people and try to figure out the nature of their relationship and what the topic of conversation is about. The trick is to get all this just by watching body language. Once you have a good idea about who they are, how they know each other and what they're talking about then politely interrupt and ask them if you were right.

Beauty

Physics captures it with the math

And poetry with words

True beauty is ephemeral

So few will ever know

The most abstract things are the most beautiful, but to appreciate them requires a certain vocabulary. This special language is responsible for the love/hate relationship people have with poetry and physics. The job of poetry is to take the experiences of life and deliver them such a way that the experiences transcend the meaning of the words. You are supposed to feel the meaning of good poetry, not just read the words.

With physics, the math is only there to explain the relationships between the phenomena in the universe, but you don't NEED the math to appreciate the way the universe works. It's just useful for explaining certain things that one can only experience. Gravity and sadness are alike this way. We have a language to describe both, but in the end, you don't NEED the language to experience them. But if you want to transmit your understanding to another person, you need to capture it with something. Ultimately math and words are the set of symbols for accomplishing just that.

Actionable Advice

Take time to enjoy the beauty that you do not immediately grasp. Music, poetry, art, writing, mathematics, etc. There are various methods to capture the human experience and one of them will strike you beyond the superficial meaning of the symbols used for expression. It won't be about the notes, or words or the formulas. Whatever you choose will be about the feelings and nothing else.

Control

When you can make slow movements fast

And fast movements slow

You've reached a level of mastery

That few ever know

Control is the ultimate goal. You start with a low level of skill and then eventually you can do a thing better than most of the world. Everyone focuses on being fast. Speed is a great attribute, but control is a better one. You're more valuable as an athlete if you have agility and mobility along with straight line speed and quickness. You spend less time drafting a letter if you type at a slower speed but have fewer errors that require correction.

Eventually, you realize that going fast and making mistakes takes longer than going slow flawlessly. There are times where it is beneficial to be faster and times when it's beneficial to be slower. You don't know exactly when those moments will be. All you can do is develop control over yourself so that you can adapt to all challenges.

Actionable Advice

Control is a display of understanding. If you take the time to demonstrate that you understand a thing, then you can use it no matter what the occasion. In your craft, there is something that you would like to know. Or perhaps there is something that you would like to know better. Begin spending time diving deeply into the subject.

If it's a physical task, break down those who have mastered it and start learning from the ground up. Gradually add layers to your understanding and you eventually will have a deeper level of understanding. This deep form of understanding manifests itself as control.

CHAPTER SIX
Paradigm Shift

Happiness comes from stretching your limits.

There are many definitions of happiness. All make valid points. I won't go over them here, nor will I attempt to add my own. Instead, I give credit to Scott Adams for this definition of happiness and how it relates to movement.

Adams says that you can't be happy unless you are moving towards a goal. Attainment of the goal is a temporary high. Overcoming the struggle is where it's at. You will always need something to force you to grow if you want to be happy. There must always be a mountain to climb because happiness is in scaling the mountain; not in reaching the apex.

Actionable Advice

The military has a saying: "Embrace the suck." This is a mantra to help endure an unpleasant task. Since you can't get out of doing the task, there is no point in complaining about it. Instead, you should embrace the awful work with enthusiasm. While this was originally coined as a coping mechanism, the brilliance behind it is that it unlocks the secret of happiness.

Happiness is not found in the completion of an unpleasant task, but rather in the task itself. Even something as unpleasant as scrubbing the urinal can be a source of happiness if you embrace the process and lose yourself in it. I can't tell you how many times guys have told me they have the most interesting revelations during miserable military tasks. Whether your task is enjoyable or miserable, embrace it wholeheartedly to experience happiness.

Not Caring What Other People Think Is A Super Power

Freedom isn't the ability to do whatever you want. Freedom is to be free from dependency on things.

It's impossible to do whatever you want. For your more malicious urges, there are laws. For your benign urges, there are limitations of time and money. You don't exist alone in this world so you will have to make compromises with the other human beings on this planet.

The degree of those compromises depends on the nature of the relationship, but every day in every way, you face restrictions on the "freedoms" you enjoy. Therefore, it is ridiculous to define freedom as the ability to do whatever you want. If this were the case, most of us would never be free.

These rules only apply to the physical realm. Even if someone removes your physical freedom, you still have your mental freedom. Through training and discipline, this ensures that your emotional freedom will also remain. The only way to experience freedom is to prevent anything from taking hold of your mind and forcing it to be dependence.

This means that you must be aware of thoughts and emotions that force you to be dependent on the outside world for validation. Jealousy, envy, and insecurity are chains for your mind that bind you to the approval of others. It is only with a free mind that you are successfully able to take on the world.

Actionable Advice:

Make a list of two or three things about your life that

you're grateful for. It doesn't matter what they are. The only thing that matters is that they bring you joy when you think about them. Once you have decided on these items, your goal is to go an entire day without succumbing to anger. You will buffer any potential anger by thinking of the things that bring you joy.

We all experience frustrations and annoyances throughout the day, but we don't have to let them be more than a blip on the emotional radar. When you find yourself experiencing anything that takes you to a negative place, remember the things that bring you immense happiness and joy. You are now exercising your right to choose your mental state. This is freedom.

Your good habits protect you from the collateral damage of other people's bad habits.

Habits are either constructive or destructive. They either make your life easier or more difficult. They accomplish this by putting behaviors on auto-pilot. Good behaviors protect and improve. Bad behaviors expose and degenerate.

When the behavior is on auto-pilot, you become a slave to it. This is why it's so important to build a set of constructive habits because they make success as easier to attain. By making it nearly automatic, much of the effort is removed.

There is another benefit of building good habits. Each good habit reduces the amount of space you have to develop a bad habit. Every good habit you have not only protects against other people's bad habits, but it protects against your own bad habits as well.

Actionable Advice

There's a bad habit you wish to break. You have probably tried many methods before so you have nothing to lose trying this one. Whatever your bad habit is, you're going to replace it with a good, but simple, habit. Every time you want to smoke a cigarette, take a walk. When you are going to watch internet porn, instead do push-ups.

You can't just get rid of a habit—you have to replace it with something else. Your mental space abhors a vacuum so it will naturally begin filling the vacated space with something. The new good habit is designed to fill that space. It won't instantly relieve you of your desire to do the bad habit, but it will help. Also, it adds a constructive activity to your day.

Approach what is easy as if it were hard and what is hard as if it were easy.

Tasks that appear difficult make you hesitate with self-doubt. You proceed in spite of yourself, hoping to survive until the end. Tasks that appear simple make you hesitate in overconfidence. Procrastination and unfulfilled ambition is the end result if you do not hi-jack this process.

Changing how you see the task is often all it takes. Viewing what's easy as difficult can spur you to take action. The satisfaction you'll get from completing that task will provide sufficient momentum. Likewise, if you view difficult things as easy, when you see them you are able to maintain the playful nature necessary to keep a fresh mind while tackling difficult projects.

Actionable Advice

The next time you are tempted to procrastinate, attack the most difficult part of the task. If the task is singular and apparently simple, imagine that you don't have enough time to complete it. Think of all the things that could go wrong to prevent you from completing the task. If imagining all the reasons you'll fail doesn't spur you into action, the task isn't important enough to motivate you.

When faced with a difficult and important task, attack the easiest part first. All difficult problems have multiple parts to them. This is one of the reasons the problem is difficult. Attacking the easiest parts first gives you confidence that you can attack the bigger pieces. Especially as you observe the scope of the task actively diminish. This bestows upon you the confidence necessary to push on.

The truth is never complicated. What's complicated is accepting how simple it really is.

The reasons why people act are very simple. People act in their own interest (extended to immediate family) first and then in the interest of those around them. This isn't good or bad, but there are pros and cons that must be understood.

While there are enlightened individuals who act with the greater good of humanity in mind, you probably aren't dealing with that type of individual. Mathematically speaking, it's far more likely that you're dealing with an average human being. If you're lucky, you may possibly be dealing with a slightly above average person.

This means their behavior can be summed up in this fashion: It isn't malicious. It isn't cruel. It isn't stupid. It's just self-centered. Your interpretation of the action doesn't change what motivated it. We have trouble accepting this simple view because we want to believe that other people are acting with our specific interests in mind. Either they want to help us or hurt us. The reality is that most of the time, they don't care. This is a simple truth that is difficult to accept.

Actionable Advice

Assume everyone is out for themselves. When you look at human behaviors this way, a lot of things you attach emotions like "cruel" or "greedy" to appear for what they really are: people doing what's in their best self-interest. If other people get hurt in the process, it doesn't mean that was the goal. Other people were just collateral damage.

When a person commits a wrong against you, remember that they aren't specifically targeting you. Rather, they are self-interested and nothing else matters. People are often accused of cruelty when they are only guilty of extreme selfishness.

Fame: People's willingness to spend time and money to experience you.

In the internet era, everyone feels like they're famous. This stems from the illusion of connectivity. A person says a thing or posts a picture, it gets a lot of likes, and the person feels important to many. While this is only an illusion, it is a remarkably persistent one. Aside from the sheer number of fans and followers that truly famous people have, they possess another distinguishing characteristic.

Fame makes people willing to spend money or time. You can't claim to be famous within a particular niche if you can't make a living teaching, entertaining, or speaking to colleagues and peers. The only measure of fame that matters is the one that lines your pocketbook. Everything else is--at best--a high school popularity contest; at worst--notoriety.

Actionable Advice

The best way to avoid "internet God" syndrome is to never lose focus of the relationships you've built over time and in person. Realizing the importance and meaning of these relationships inoculates you against inflating the importance of your internet presence.

It's hard to get angry at things you see on the internet when your actual life is great and full of meaning. If you legitimately do become famous, you will hardly notice because your personal relationships are so meaningful that ones you digitally forged with strangers will have little meaning.

Not Caring What Other People Think Is A Super Power

Knowledge without action is the same as ignorance.

Simply knowing a thing is useless. How you use the knowledge is all that matters. One hour of action is worth more than all the knowledge in a library. The only way we can tell a person is ignorant is if they do things that reveal their lack of knowledge. We can't tell just by looking at them. Having a mind full of theoretical knowledge is no different than ignorance if you still lead a mediocre life.

Actionable Advice

There is great value in knowing exactly how something works, but there is even greater value in knowing what it can't do. All things, including ourselves, have limitations. Part of complete knowledge is awareness of these limitations. Theoretical knowledge does not give one the lasting lessons in their personal limitations and how to overcome them. Real experience does.

Your task is to pick a skill you want to learn more about. You can read one primer on it and then you are to make as many mistakes as you can over the next 30 days. Any skill will suffice. For example, building a website, trying a new sport, learning a new language or even learning chess. Just be reasonable about the risks you'll accept. Getting skinned knees is fine but losing the rent money probably isn't a worthwhile risk-reward proposition.

Giving unsolicited advice is surprisingly useless and mostly for entertainment. We learn the longest lasting lessons the "hard way".

When you give someone advice, you have to remember something: everyone believes they will be the exception. Don't take their disobedience personally. In the interest of reducing the stress in your life, don't invest too much in what you tell people.

Many people have to learn things the hard way. People also make decisions based on emotions and support it with facts later. In this way, they can make themselves feel better about even the dumbest decision. Ultimately, there are few people that will actually take your advice.

Of the people that will take it, almost none of them will actually ask you because they are busy correcting their own problems. Therefore, most of the advice you give is useless. Even the people who do ask are mainly hoping for confirmation of a decision they've already made. If the advice you give is in opposition of what they've decided, most times they won't entertain your opinion.

Actionable Advice

You must learn to be unattached to the outcome of things in general. Specifically, you must learn to detach yourself from the outcomes of other people's actions. From now on, cease giving unsolicited advice. This will solve most of your problems in this area. Even if a person specifically asks you for your advice, your default response is "You should do whatever feels right."

The only time you should invest your time in giving someone proper advice is when they are adamantly trying things but can't seem to catch a break. Look for self-starting effort and a strong initiative to correct their own problems. Even when you give advice, give without expectation of them following through and let the event take no space in your mind.

Having more money never hurts. Having less money never helps.

Almost every problem in your life can be solved by having more money. At the very least, those problems become significantly easier to manage. There is a popular saying that is the opposite: "Mo money, mo problems." This is only true for people that have a host of other problems. Money does not change a person or their external circumstances. What money does is amplify what is already there.

The mentality and habits that make a person rich or poor are only increased by the freedom that money brings. If you have bad habits, you'll have more problems. If you have good habits, you'll have more solutions. Having more money never hurts. Having less money never helps.

Actionable Advice

You may become rich. You may not. That's entirely up to you. This isn't a tutorial on how to get wealthy. However, your attitudes have an effect on not only the likelihood of you making money, but on the likelihood of you keeping it as well. I won't list every habit that is likely to contribute to your financial ruin, but I will discuss a particularly dangerous mindset.

If you gain your sense of worth from external objects and recognition, you'll have trouble keeping a large amount of your money. Also, if you do not have the ability to delay gratification, you will have a much smaller chance of making money or keeping it.

If you recognize that your weakness is needing to buy things to feel better or alter your mood, then the next step is learning to find value in what you accomplish. If you cannot delay gratification, then you will use money to satisfy your immediate urges instead of considering the long term. Even if you don't become extremely wealthy, these habits will improve your quality of life.

If you can take the complex and make it simple for people to understand, there's a lot of money for you somewhere.

There are people in this world that make lots of money by taking what appears to be difficult and making it seem simple. The idea of any diet pill or life hack is that it's taking something difficult and making it seem easy. How you feel about these industries and their practices are irrelevant.

What is relevant is what these industries actually represent. They convince people that there is an easier way to do something difficult. Everyone wants an easy way to gain the benefits that follow the most difficult of accomplishments, but strength built from enduring the journey is what actually admired.

Actionable Advice

Observe all the ways the world tries to sell you shortcuts. Every course for learning, every dating app, diet pill, and most pieces of exercise equipment are all marketed as the easiest way to do something. You must train yourself to see this trick in play.

When a product is claiming that it will reduce the amount of time or effort it takes to do a task that will improve you, you know that it is almost certainly a sham. This works because the average person looks for the easiest path to something. Because of this attitude, they will never accomplish their given aim.

Reject all things that promise an easy shortcut. However, if your plan is to sell things, play on the fact that the average person is not interested in doing hard work. They want what is simple and easy. Oblige them.

Every moment spent consuming is a moment lost producing.

The quickest way to improve your life is to increase your value. The quickest way to increase your value is to begin producing and contributing to the world.

Most people are consumers. They slave through the days of the week and drink the nights and the weekends away. They don't improve because they consume the worst the world has to offer in terms of food and information. When you spend your time consuming, you don't have enough value to exchange for the good stuff life has to offer. Excessive consumption depreciates the mind and body, making it essentially worthless.

Your goal is to become a producer. You want to add value to the world. By putting high quality into your body and mind, it is able to create the best. What you create and contribute increases your worth. By increasing your worth, everything you consume has a finer quality and the cycle continues upwards. But you cannot produce and consume simultaneously. Some consumption is necessary for your life and enjoyment, but you should produce far more than you consume.

Actionable Advice

Your goal is to produce something in the next 30 days. What you produce has to be something that can stand alone. It doesn't have to be perfect, but it does have to be complete. For example, a manuscript is complete when the first draft is finished although it is far from perfect. A program is complete when it can do the task it was built for, even if it is not debugged and optimized.

Produce something that can go forth and add value to the world without you, even if it is on a shaky foundation.

The difference between poor and broke is the mindset. Broke is temporary and can be fixed. Poor is a quality of mind that affects your whole life.

Broke and poor are as different as wet and dry. Broke is the result of an event. Poor is the result of a mindset. Broke is recognizing your funds are low, but working to change this. Poor is accepting your bank account as an unalterable part of your identity.

I know poor people with money but they are incredibly paranoid, sloppy, emotionally unstable individuals. Broke people always sleep well at night. Money is very important but it is not who you are and it can't make you someone you're not.

Actionable Advice

Assess your true net worth. This is independent of the money you have in the bank. While everyone thinks they want to have a lot of money, what really matters is your state of mind. If you don't leverage your cash to give yourself greater peace of mind, you will always be poor.

Peace of mind is not found in the latest gadgets, fashionable clothing, in the biggest house or even on the nicest vacation. These things are enjoyable, but they don't release you from the mindset of a poor person. Neither does having a bunch of cash saved in the bank. This is important, but not for the reasons you think. The only thing that matters is how you can use the money to create an environment that strengthens your relationships.

This means that the big house isn't important so much as the safety it allows you to provide your children. The vacation isn't important if it's just mindless consumption that doesn't improve you or your relationships. Gadgets and clothing are at best worthless and at worst, liabilities. This is what poor people don't understand.

The value of life is found in other people. Money facilitates your relationship with people but it is by no means necessary. There are many people around the world that don't have a lot of money, but they are not poor because they have strong relationships.

Focus on building your relationships. Use money strengthen them. That is all that matters. That is how you move from poor to rich.

Motion is the best way to get out of a funk. Use your body, have a conversation, get busy. Stagnation keeps you in your mind.

Controlling your mind can be difficult. This difficulty arises from a misunderstanding of the human organism. The mind and the body are interconnected. The mind moves the body and the body provides feedback to the mind based on what it encounters. When we experience negative moods, a powerful and simple remedy is to change our movement.

Just making the motion of a smile can improve your mood while having stagnant and stiff posture can make you anxious. When you are depressed and down in the dumps, do something that involves movement. It gets your thoughts in motion and takes the focus off of the sinking feeling you have in your body. It won't fix what's wrong—only handing the actual problem can do that—but it will provide temporary relief.

Actionable Advice

When you feel yourself getting angry, take a walk. A good walk clears the mind because it gets you moving. This walk is likely spontaneous, but if it isn't, do not take any music. Just start moving. If you can't start walking, imagine you're walking and telling a joke. You may not laugh, but you definitely should smile. The motion of the smile is power. Imagining that you're walking is powerful. These are all methods used to shake you out of a funk.

It's not what you don't know that hurts you. It's what you thought was so but isn't true that does the most damage.

Not all mistruths are created equal. Certain lies make you invest a large amount of time and energy in a path that will not work out. If you were given honest information about the situation you would have easily seen this, but alas you were misled.

Omitting information can have this effect, but it is far less likely to because often times the omission of information leads to continuation of prior actions. Nothing really changes. But when you are actively feed disinformation, that is when the real damage is done.

It is beautiful to use minimum words for maximum expression.

If you have to use a lot of words to communicate your idea, your idea will be lost. People have short attention spans so they will get bored. You also risk being misunderstood because you aren't communicating directly. Extra words dilute the original message until it is unrecognizable.

Actionable Advice

For the next week, only give yes and no answers to questions. Do not elaborate unless necessary. If you have to explain a concept for professional reasons or there is a serious personal situation, this is an obvious exception. This exercise is for the times you feel the need to explain yourself unnecessarily. Many people are not comfortable with being succinct. This is why so many people "beat around the bush." If you're one of those people, this will be an uncomfortable change.

You also are not permitted to engage in small talk. Every conversation you have must be to learn something. This can be as casual as learning whether a girl will go out with you (you ask her directly) or regarding something professional. No matter what, small talk about trivial or unrelated matters is forbidden for the week.

Gain a reputation for ruthlessness and you can be kind. Gain a reputation for kindness and you will be the target of ruthlessness.

When you have a reputation for being tough, people will be wary of you. They are less likely to take advantage of you. When people know that you are kind, they are more likely to take advantage of you. This isn't as malicious as it seems. It's simply the result of human beings doing what they do best: taking the path of least resistance.

This is why you can't afford to be known as kind. You will have more work with less of a pay off because you'll constantly have to deal with people trying to take advantage of you. If you are known as a hard ass, then people are less likely to waste your time trying to get something for nothing.

Actionable Advice

Say no. If you can learn to say no to people when they make a request of you, people will be less likely to make requests of you. This is a good thing because it means that there will be fewer demands on your physical and mental energy.

It also means that people will have greater respect for you. This is because it automatically makes you more selective in who you give your time to. When people know that you give your time to anyone, they are less likely to respect it. Saying no to most requests and inquiries of your personal time increases the respect others have for you.

The world isn't boring. You are.

I'm not going to make a complete list of all the things you could do in the world. I'm not even going to make a partial list. This would be like giving you a fish instead of teaching you how to fish. Actually, it'd be even less productive because what if you don't like fish at all? What if you already know how to fish but you're just lazy? What if you have no inclination towards learning how to fish at all and would rather hunt or farm? Instead of giving you my ideas on how to alleviate boredom, I will tell you what boredom is and its antithesis. The rest is up to you.

Boredom is a lack of fascination. You may lack interest, it may not be interesting, or you may be intimately knowledgeable of the thing. Why you aren't fascinated is irrelevant. What is relevant is understanding that boredom is the lack of interest in something. Recognize this when you experience the feeling.

The opposite of boring is interesting. Children are rarely bored because everything in the world is new and novel. It is all so interesting to them. People who are deeply engaged in something cease to experience boredom because they are acting in a meaningful way rather than just going through the motions. When deeply focused on an experience to the point where you notice the minor nuances of a thing, fascination begins and boredom ends.

Actionable Advice

Learn to meditate. You don't need to become a professional, but you do need to learn how to focus within yourself. By learning how to make your mind aware and active internally, you are also learning how to become fascinated with yourself. Not only do you discover many things about yourself, but you also learn how to control your mind. Since boredom begins in the mind, it is only sensible to begin training the mind first in order to conquer it.

It doesn't matter if the glass is half empty or half full; the glass is refillable.

No matter how good or how bad your situation seems, harbor no attachments for fortunes are suspended by a pendulum. While pendulums oscillate by their own momentum, they do require an initial push.

This push can come at any time from any direction. There are no limitations. It doesn't matter how good or bad the pendulum's position is; what matters is that it can—and will—change direction. Its situation is not fixed, for better or worse. Its fortune is mutable.

Actionable Advice

When a situation is going well, practice gratitude and remember how bad life can be otherwise. When a situation is going badly, remember how good life has been before. Know that whatever you are feeling, it will pass. Hold no attachment to the good or bad situations because, ultimately, they all swing back to their opposite. This is the way of life.

Not Caring What People Think Is Damn Near A Super Power.

You're only as powerful as your darkest secret. You must remember that shame's power is only in your imagination. It's not a gun to your head. It's not your family being held hostage. The only potential victim is your pride. Pride is how the ego holds itself together. Often your ego is a good thing. It is how you define yourself and it gives you the mental fortitude to resist the influences of the world. This is also the ego's greatest weakness.

Anything that contradicts the image it holds for itself is deemed a threat. You believe yourself to be one way, but there are things you have done that makes your ego think of itself a different way. As long as you can bury these dark secrets of cognitive dissonance, your ego and self-image remain complete. You feel safe.

The moment someone threatens to show the world what you and your ego really are, then you are threatened. Then, in the interest of self-preservation, you'll do whatever it takes to alleviate the pressure. At best, this means you'll cave to social pressures. At worst, you are shamed and blackmailed into doing someone's bidding. This is how sharp individuals are dulled down to the level of their surroundings. They want to be perceived a certain way by the masses so they mute the things about them that would make them incredible. Societal approval is the invisible force crushing the greatness out of everyone that succumbs to it. The only defense against this is not giving a damn what anyone thinks.

No special confidence is required for this. No initial level of achievement is needed. All one must do is embrace their individuality. Most of us are trained to think a certain way when we're children. As we grow we carry these thought patterns, for better and for worse. Caring about what people think keeps you from doing stuff that hurts people and breaks the law. That's a positive. It also keeps you from taking good risks that will put you in a position to achieve great success. That's the negative.

The reason? Fear. Your ego personally fears that it will be unmasked and that you aren't really as great as you think. It's one thing to believe it in a bubble, but it's a different game entirely when you have to test your ideas against harsh reality. Others shame you into conformity because if you succeed, then it reminds them of their own failure. Their ego sees that while the risk is scary and that destruction (failure is always destruction to the ego) is possible, so is new birth and creation. Other egos don't want this revealed, so they stamp down any that will show this is possible.

You want to create. The masses want you to consume. Even though the immense freedom and power that you'd have is obvious, the system of ego's keeps you down. The only way to defeat them is to develop your super power of apathy. If you don't care what the masses think then you're damn near invincible. There is something you must understand: The best prison isn't physical. It's mental. It's fortified by your fears, guarded by your insecurities and funded by public shame. Almost every person you meet serves a function in this jail. Most are inmates, some are guards and a few are wardens.

Once you break free, there is nothing they can do to

bring you back. Now you rule the roost. You are free to do whatever you please in the world, provided it doesn't land in a physical prison. This a superhuman level of freedom that most never experience. To truly not care what anyone thinks isn't damn near a super power. In these times, it is one.

CHAPTER SEVEN
Strategy and Tactics

Strategy without tactics is the slowest route to victory. Tactics without strategy is the noise before defeat.

Strategy is the big picture. The view from on high. The plan you'd like to execute. Tactics are the moment to moment actions. The view from within the battle. Tactics are the exact methods you'll use to accomplish your plan. In the military, the strategy is usually left up to the officers to plan while the tactics are executed by the enlisted soldiers. In the workplace, the strategy is planned by the upper management and CEOs. The tactics are executed by lower management and the employees under them.

In fighting, the strategy is a game plan you have for neutralizing an opponent. Tactics are the attacks and movements you'll use to do so. The examples could continue indefinitely but the idea is the same—strategy is the mission and tactics are the methods used to bolster advantages and exploit weaknesses.

It's possible to be excellent at one, lacking in another, and still have success. There are sports teams with great players and a mediocre coach that couldn't win with any other group. Likewise, there are great coaches that take an unspectacular team and makes them great.

The coach is the strategist and the players are the tacticians. A good coach without strong players may eventually have success, but it will come at a high cost over a long time. Likewise, a mediocre coach with exceptionally talented players may get the team a lot of attention, but they never win the big game. Any reader that is a fan of sports can find numerous examples of this playing out. Strategy without tactics is the long way to the top. Tactics without strategy is entertaining but ultimately will fail.

Simulated disorder postulates perfect discipline. Simulated fear postulates courage. Simulated weakness postulates strength.

A vaccine works by infecting you with a weak enough version of the virus that your body creates antibodies capable of defending against the stronger version. Only by exposing yourself to a component of something are you able to develop the proper tools to deal with it on a larger scale. No matter how much running you do for conditioning, nothing gets you in shape for boxing like boxing. That's what sparring is for—to simulate the fighting in a controlled scenario so that you are prepared for it when there are no restrictions.

Learning to survive in the simulated disorder requires a high level of discipline. Functioning in a low level of fear builds the courage to perform in the face of something that is immensely terrifying. Training with restrictions to weaken you will develop strength for when you perform without them.

A theoretical disadvantage that can't be exploited by your opponent is not really a weakness at all.

In competition your success depends on two things— how good you are and how good your opponent is. This seems obvious but let's consider the implications. It means there are guys that you beat because you are better than them and guys that you beat because they either don't exploit or recognize a disadvantage you have.

Therefore, the best they can do is force a draw or—or as we understand when strategy lacks effective tactics— hope for a slow and most likely pyrrhic victory. Your disadvantages aren't really disadvantages if your opponent doesn't understand how to exploit them.

There's a direct correlation between how much time you consider before an action and its likelihood of success.

The primary difference between strategy and tactics is the amount of time and space you must take into consideration before execution. A tactic is short term and often reactionary. A strategy is long-term and as such—by definition—can not be in immediate reaction to anything. It's impossible to have a short term strategy. That's just a tactic. You can have success on strategy alone. It might take a long time, but it is possible.

You will not have lasting success relying on tactics alone. There is too much variability from moment to moment. If you're spending most of your time reacting and figuring out the best moves for what just happened, you'll never be in a position to deal with future problems in a clear state of mind. You'll have far fewer successes and fulfill less of your potential.

Strategy, by its very nature, forces you to look into the future. Therefore, the superior strategy will consider a greater amount of time before selecting a suitable plan of action. Because more time or space is considered, one is able to figure out the most effective tactics to apply to the situation.

Live strategically, with a view from high. Avoid tactical hell (reacting to everything).

Most people are good at tactical living. We are excellent at surviving the day to day grind. Living paycheck to paycheck is tactical living. Only going to the doctor when sick is tactical living. Only having discussions about relationship problems whilst arguing is tactical living. You'll survive, you'll live, but you'll never be great.

Living below your means, saving money and planning to make more, engaging in preventive checkups and health practices, regularly talking things over in your relationship. This is how you stay ahead of the routine problems in life that demolish you in a tactical assault. This is how you start attacking life strategically. Once you start living strategically, avoiding tactical hell, your entire life will improve.

The man who knows how will always have a job. The man that knows why will always be his boss.

Who is more valuable to your daily life? An electrical engineer or an electrician? A software engineer or the computer technician? The CEO of your supermarket or the employees you interact with every day? They're both important, but one group has a rarer skill set than the other. Not only is it rare, but the knowledge that comes with that skill set makes it possible for their counterparts have a job.

An electrician is useless without a functional power grid. The tech at Geek Squad (and the sales reps for all your computer products) would be out of a job if that incredible software wasn't designed. No matter how great and helpful the customer service is, they wouldn't be there to help you if the CEO tanked the company.

Knowing why something works allow you to move to the top of the food chain in any endeavor. There are guys coaching that can throw certain punches but don't know why. They will only be able to make their student as good as they are lucky. I encountered many coaching situations like this, where I was merely told how I should move my body with the hopes that magically I'd arrive at a deeper understanding. It wasn't until I had a series of coaches who could explain why I should do certain things that I developed.

When you can explain "why" you inadvertently pick up the "how". When you just know "how", there's no guarantee you can teach someone else. People will always need to know why. If you only know how, you're as disposable as the amount of time it takes to teach you how to be useful.

Always improve technical fundamentals, but make them fit your style. Not vice versa. This is why the best are always specialists.

We are all beginners in the same way. It is only when we reach mastery do styles emerge. Any complex skill will always produce different styles at the top levels. This happens because there are a set of fundamental ideas that everyone participating must understand.

In boxing, everyone learns the jab. In no-limit poker, we all learn not to bet with 2-7 off suit. In chess, we all learn the basics of opening play. People that don't learn these skills are eventually beaten out by those that do. For the ones that do, an interesting question arises: how do you gain an edge when everyone flawlessly executes the basics?

This is the next level where individual preferences arise. When everyone can throw punches with proficiency, then they figure out which ones they have a preference for. This becomes the punch with which they build world class ability. An entire fighting system and personality is developed around the skills and abilities that a person takes beyond proficiency.

Once the fundamentals in poker are learned, some players become very aggressive while others transform into patient boa constrictors that slowly squeeze the money out of you. They can do this because the fundamentals are so ingrained they no longer require thought. It is not until you know the rules that you can confidently break them. These deviations and preferences are called styles.

Always play the long game. Make moves based on the next 3 years, not the next 3 days.

Living in the future is not a bad thing. The problem is having no plan to make the future a reality. That's daydreaming. To successfully live in the future, everything you do today has to be focused on what you want tomorrow. This is the benefit of delayed gratification and strategic thinking.

It forces you to imagine where you want your life to be and then to work backward and ruthlessly eliminate anything that will not get you there. Anything that does not get you closer to your goal is a distraction. Some distractions are so enticing you may chase them instead. Sometimes this is fine but mostly it is a matter of a weak mind, low self-discipline, and giving into immediate gratification.

Your weaknesses are only weaknesses when you fail to use them to your advantage.

For your inadequacies you have three choices: improve them, ignore them, or use them to your advantage. Most times we'll choose the first option. The second is the last resort. Ideally, we'd always take the final choice. My favorite athletes to follow and read about are the ones who are physically subpar for their sport but go on to have incredibly dominant careers. They were able to do this by making their lack of physical ability an advantage rather than a disadvantage.

The poker players that present the greatest danger in a tournament are those with just enough chips to survive a few rounds of antes so they're waiting to pick their shot to go all in. This move is effective and it takes their disadvantage (a small stack) and turns it into an advantage. Almost every perceived weakness can be a point of strength if you are creative enough.

Mastery. A satisfying feeling when one finally gets on top of a new set of skills only to realize they allow him to learn even more.

In chess, one is only a considered a master after meeting a certain rating and requirements. It doesn't make the player even close to the best in the world, but it does recognize that he is superior to most players who are in various beginner stages. Thus, the master chess player still has many things to learn. Mastery begins at the point where you know enough to be better than most but a lot less than the best.

Good fighters take advantage of mistakes. Great ones make you make them.

The best competitors are so tactically proficient that reacting to things in real time is automatic to them. They don't have to think about what the best response is to anything because their tactical database is complete. Without thinking, they know the weaknesses in your position and the mistakes you'll make.

This means they don't spend any more time in the present—instead, they start figuring out ways to cause you mistakes in the future. Their game becomes about setting traps and forcing mistakes. Setting traps is an advanced skill because it means you no longer have to be present in the moment because the moment is now a part of you.

After you spend years learning, your goal is to forget. Simplicity and economy are the only way to the next level.

We start out not knowing what we don't know. Then we know what we don't know. Then we know enough and this surge of knowledge makes us think we know it all. The final level is when you've developed the humility that comes from experience. It's the humility that comes from knowing that there is still much you don't know.

This is a very good place to be, but ultimately one must reach the fifth level. You must forget everything you've learned and operate on feel alone. This refined feeling requires no thought. Only being. Thinking takes time. Reacting—while faster—takes time. When you operate on feel, you are always where you need to be the moment you need to be there. Forgetting technique is the way to transcend speed. You can't skip to this step because to forget a thing, you must know it first.

If you focus on the process, superior outcomes are a certainty. If you focus on the outcome, you'll skip important parts of the process.

Process-oriented thinking keeps you focused on the steps and procedures required to ensure a particular outcome. Nothing is guaranteed in life. All you can do is stack the odds in your favor. Each step done correctly and with diligence increases your chances of success. If you focus only on the outcome you increase the possibility that you will fail because you aren't focused on the foundational steps that support your goal.

There is another important reason to focus on processes instead of outcomes. Everyone desires the same basic outcomes. We all want money, to be attractive, to have attractive people like this, to be healthy and to be happy. If you focus only on the outcome, you might do something like rob a bank, or go on a crash diet, or develop detrimental habits to make people like you. These are short term solutions that focus only on the outcome. They do nothing for the transformative process that you must endure to attain the things you want. A positive outcome is often the unintended benefit of a diligent process.

A general strategy is good, but one must be dynamic and detached if he wants to see all tactical possibilities for victory.

Despite the fact that we must consider a large amount of time and space to form an effective strategy, the conditions of the battle field are not static. The best strategy is one that can be abandoned for its superior at a moment's notice.

Tactical opportunities present themselves in such a way that only the foolish would not take advantage of them. In order to do so, you often must change your strategy. Surprise short term difficulties may have a similar effect. In this way, the best strategy is a flexible mind that can spot all opportunities and a spirit that can creatively manipulate them to your advantage.

Tactics before strategy is the best route to mastery. You need to have control of the brush strokes before you can paint the bigger picture.

In chess, it is said that until your rating is 1800, most of your games will be decided by tactics. It took me a while to understand why this is or even what it means, but ultimately I came to understand this through boxing. Having great technique in boxing will allow you to do a lot of damage and defend effectively. You can go far and even win a title this way. This is because human beings respond to pain and being able to punch well and keep yourself from getting hit leverages this fact in your favor. But when two guys meet with equal technical skill, the victor will be the one that understands positioning, timing, and initiative—all strategic concepts.

Tactical ability is what allows a competitor to take advantage of moments they spot. These moments open up because of strategic planning. This is why, generally speaking, matches are lost based on lack of tactical merit. Good tacticians are very good at spotting what opens up in the short term. They lack the ability to see how things may change over large amounts of space and time. Likewise, a master painter is not just good at maneuvering the brush strokes for a specific effect—he sees the whole picture in his mind while making skilled strokes.

There are so many analogies between boxing, poker, and chess. They're physical, mental and emotional disciplines that mirror each other.

Boxing uses gloves in a ring, poker uses cards at a table, and chess uses the mind at a board. Ignore the medium of these complex tasks. If you only look at the surface, there are almost no similarities. It's only when you dig deeper into the subtle mechanisms that drive each discipline that you see each is an analogy for the other in interesting ways.

There are many times I have taken my understanding from one discipline and linked it to another. The point is not that boxing, poker, and chess have subtle similarities. The point is that life has subtle similarities! Train your mind to work together to see them. Then you can pull gems of understanding from the world around you and apply it to your specific problem.

You can go far in anything if you master the basics.

Every complex skill is made up of fundamental components. These are the first things you learn in route to mastery of a subject. Often times, a person stifles their development by falling in love with a particular trait that gives them a unique advantage. This unique advantage will take them far, but not nearly as far as if they had mastered the complete set of fundamentals.

In competition, you don't rise to the occasion but fall to the level of your training. If you lack fundamentals and the advantage you've relied upon for so long is unexpectedly neutralized, you will have great difficulty competing. However, if you spend the extra time needed to become well rounded and build a strong base, you will be much harder to neutralize and you will have many more successes.

Your competitor's vulnerabilities must be exploited. You should expect the same treatment from him as well.

The whole idea of a fight is that you are trying to win.While there may be certain rules you have to abide by, your goal is still to win. This means that you must take advantage of any opening, inadequacy or weakness.

A fair fight means all things are equally possible. This is not only in your worst interest as a competitor, but it is impossible. If everything were equal, then no one could win. Your goal must be to stack the odds of victory significantly in your favor. If you're in a fair fight that means you're doing something wrong.

Be proactive so you don't have to be reactive.

The best defense is a good offense. If your opponent has to constantly deal with your assault, then he has no time to mount his own. While this requires a large amount of energy and initiative, you still have the advantage in time and space by acting first.

When you force someone to react, then you know what they're going to do before they do. This peek into the future gives you a tremendous advantage. By making your opponent do what you want them to do, they'll have no time to enforce their will on the situation.

Becoming a true strategist is effectively gaining the power to see the future.

When you see things with a strategic eye, you are no longer concerned with the immediate present. This is because you have already planned for the moment you are in. Your mind is free to consider the next chunk of time and space.

There are times you will feel like you are looking into the future. Things happen that seem to baffle other people but you are fully prepared for them. You look like a better tactician because you know what is possible, the likelihood of it, and how to handle it. This is the power of becoming a true strategist.

CHAPTER EIGHT

Relationships

Men are simple. What's complicated is accepting how simple they really are.

Both men and women are complicated. The difference between men and women is the transparency of our basic motivations. Men's desires are easily quantifiable and tangible. Men are motivated by how much they can control and influence their reality. A man out of control is a man in discord with the world. Whether he is wealthy or of average means, the larger his degree of control, the better he will feel.

To make a man happy in a relationship, all that is needed is support and physical beauty. She doesn't need to be the most beautiful woman in the world, but she needs to be the most beautiful version of herself. This is easier than all the advice on how to attract a man might suggest. Men don't care about make-up or exceptional style. They care if you maintain good hygiene and are physically fit. It's very simple.

Men want a girl that is supportive and inspiring. There are many ways to be this way. If a man has an attractive partner that brightens his day, he will be inspired to move a mountain to wage a thousand wars. A supportive woman that maintains her appearance is a simple and accurate list of the demands most men have.

Actionable Advice

For men, understand that these two things determine your long term happiness and level of attraction to a woman. Therefore, it is important that you screen for them from the start. You may not know how a relationship will turn out, but if you begin with the end in mind then it's more likely that things will go well.

Only approach women that you find attractive. During the conversation, discover her general demeanor and outlook on the world. Positive, almost naively optimistic, is better than pessimistic and sarcastic.

You learn more about a couple watching them argue for 5 minutes than seeing them happy for 5 years.

Even the worst paired couple looks like a match made in heaven when things are going well. Their true compatibility is only revealed during times of disagreement. As human beings, we will always have something to disagree about. It's unreasonable to think this will ever change, yet we still manage to (mostly) co-exist.

This means that agreements and disagreements between two people are temporary conditions. As such, any judgments rendered about a couple while they are happy are at best, incomplete, and at worst, inaccurate. A complete and accurate portrait of a couple is only formed when you watch them settle a conflict.

The true test of a relationship is how fights are handled. The goal, above all others, is to strike an agreement beneficial to both sides. The benefit doesn't have to be maximal nor must it be what both sides originally intended. All that matters is that there is an improvement over the original situation and both people feel that they've gained something.

Couples focused on solving the problem approach arguments as negotiations. Couples that focus on selfish gain approach arguments like war. The victory they achieve will only be pyrrhic in nature. No couple can survive fighting in a relationship if the goal is to destroy the other person.

Actionable Advice

Adopt the negotiator's mindset. At the very least, when you have interrelationship conflict you must think about how you can make both sides win. When you think like this, it automatically keeps you focused on and more likely to achieve the main idea: to get something for both parties. By adhering to this mindset, you are more likely to emerge victoriously.

If you are only focused on defeating the other person, then your chances of victory decrease. Most disagreements aren't worth disrupting your peace of mind over. The ones where there is a position or item at stake, approach the argument with the following idea in mind: "it is better to win a little than lose it all". When in doubt, let this guide your words and actions.

When changing your manner of thinking, it is natural to go too far in the other direction. You don't want to give up your entire position. Your goal is to negotiate and compromise—not to become a doormat that gets nothing in return. There is no hard rule for what you should and shouldn't give up so you'll have to navigate this yourself. But just as your goal isn't to completely dominate the other person, it's also not to completely subjugate yourself.

Good women make you fall for them. Great women inspire you to become a man that keeps them falling for you.

A good woman does not add any stress to the life of her lover. She is pleasant and they almost never disagree. When disagreements occur, the path to resolution is peaceful and swift. While not spectacular in any way, she is not a detriment to his life or well-being.

There are many women like this in the world. There are also many bad women in the world. A man could (and usually does) do a lot worse than a good-woman. Aiming to be a good woman is not a bad goal. Most men spend their lives looking for a good woman.

On the other hand, a great woman has one thing that the good woman does not. There are many physical, mental and emotional traits that allow her to have this one thing, but it is what separates her from the women that are just good. A great woman inspires those around her. A great woman, more than anything, inspires her man.

Many men get into a relationship and consider it the finish line. Outside of doing what they need to do to excel in their chosen profession, they cease almost all behaviors that make them attractive. They coast at the level they entered the relationship at.

However, nothing in the universe is neutral so they regress until they become an unattractive shell of their former selves. The power of a great woman is that she inspires the man in her life to keep improving. In this inspiration, she also inspires him to find new and exciting ways to be attractive to her.

This is what separates the goods from the greats. The goods are relatively rare and will make a man fall for them. Sometimes they do this based on nothing more than being a better alternative to the other options. A great woman, on the other hand, makes a man want to be better every single moment. Great women attract a higher quality of man, but the man they find never regress. She is part of the reason why.

Actionable Advice

Adopt the belief that no matter what, you must always be improving. This will ensure that when you get into a relationship that you won't ever let yourself stagnate, for stagnation is death. As long as you are in the process of continual improvement, this is the standard you will judge any woman by who enters your life.

If you are improving and she is not improving, then you'll be in a better position to recognize this and thus move on to a relationship that is better suited for you.

"I'm focusing on my career, health, or some nonsense instead of trying to meet someone" is the worst excuse ever by lonely people.

There is never a right time to start a new relationship but there are a few bad times. You probably shouldn't start a new relationship if you're currently in one. Or if you're headed to prison. Outside of these situations, you can always start a new relationship.

The conditions may not be ideal, but they will never be ideal. This is because solving problems is part of what defines life. If you wait until your life is perfect to fall in love, then you will wait for an eternity.

It also implies that somehow the relationship will not add any problems to your life. This is a falsehood that many single people subconsciously believe. When you get into a relationship then you get a new person to experience a new set of problems with. While you should not neglect your problems to pursue a romantic relationship, a romantic relationship—being part of life —also presents an opportunity for new problems to arise.

The time spent building a potentially meaningful relationship does not detract from time spent developing a career or improving your health. These things often work in tandem and give you motivation. Using your problems as an excuse to stay single will ensure that you remain that way long after you solve them.

Actionable Advice

No matter what, you are always the problem. It is not other things in your life. And if somehow the other conditions are detracting but you are interested in improving your romantic life, you'll make the necessary modifications. But you have to be honest with yourself that this is what you really want.

If you aren't interested in pursuing romantic options, own that decision. If you are interested, do what you must to make it happen. But you are longer allowed to attribute anything in your life to an outside force—romantic or otherwise.

You learn just as much from being in a serious relationship as you do from playing the field. Likewise, you aren't complete until you do both.

Despite the fact that being single and playing the field require two different approaches, they both demand you understand fundamental ideas about the way men and women interact. They are different sides of the same coin. Lessons learned from your relationships as well as flings eventually make you a capable general in whichever life you chose to lead.

You may choose to have a wife and a family or you may choose to spend your days in eternal bachelorhood. Either way, you'll be equipped to handle the ups and downs that the women in your life bring. This ensures you'll be happy so that everyone around you will also be happy.

Actionable Advice

For a man to be completely happy, he must feel as if he can survive. This is not only limited to his resources. He must have confidence in his psychological abilities as well. The only way to get this confidence is through experience.

If you are not having the experiences you want with women, learn from men more experienced. You can do this in direct conversation or through their writing. Most importantly, learn from your own interactions—whether they be short or long.

Within 3 months of a new relationship, you already know what's going to break you up. If you stick around, you have no one to blame but yourself.

One of the challenges you face when starting a new relationship is learning about what makes the other person tick. When you meet someone new, your perspective is tainted by strong emotions. This has the ability to color your judgment about the true nature of the new romantic interest. This may cause you to subdue the feelings you get when when they do something contrary to our values.

In a new relationship, you know what's going to break you up. When the new emotions stabilize, the once ignorable habits become intolerable. Rarely do people change in relationships. Rarely does your tolerance change in relationships. What changes is your ability to ignore the offense.

Actionable Advice

The only way to guard yourself against the persuasive powers of a new partner's charm is to ruthlessly adhere to standards. There is a danger of becoming dogmatic with this approach and mistake slight mishaps for large grievances. The way to inoculate yourself against this is to be strict about where you draw the line, but lenient in all the things.

Having your tolerances clearly defined ahead of time will allow you to lose yourself in the pool of love because you have a lifeline to bring you back if things do not go according to plan. By letting everything else go that does not affect your standards, you can enjoy new love without worry. This is a win-win situation.

Unless you're from a city with +1 million people, expect to have a hard time dating and making new friends as you improve.

The further away you move from average, the smaller the number of people there will be that you connect with. If we look at this as a statistics problem and assume that the defining traits of a population are normally distributed, then once you are 2 standard deviations away from the mean, only 5% of the population is on your level. Once you get to 3, you find you have almost nothing in common with 99% of the population.

Let's assume that you make it two levels above the normal. This means you enjoy deep and meaningful conversations, staying in shape, live with a goal or mission, and would rather solve problems with like-minded people rather than argue over things that have nothing to do with your life. In a city of 250,000 people, there are just 12,500 people you mesh with. This might seem like a lot, but you have to remember a few things.

Many will be too young (not yet developed) or too old (not mobile or fully able) and thus not exposed to the general population. Some will be extremely busy (as people of this caliber tend to be) or occupied raising families (people of this caliber don't have a problem mating). Although there will be some venues that attract a higher portion of them, it's safe to assume that they'll be scattered amongst the city. As you improve in a city this size, you'll have fewer people that you are capable of connecting with.

In a city of at least 1 million, the numbers look a lot

better. Now you have 50,000 people to choose from. Even with all the conditions above, you still have a sizable portion of people you are likely to connect with. Because there are more like-minded people, there is a great chance there is a structure of support. This means more places they are likely to meet and a bigger network to introduce you to others. Self-improvement is often a lonely pursuit, but it doesn't have to be if you live in a place with enough like-minded individuals.

Actionable Advice

Not everyone has the means to move to a bigger city. To get an idea of how many people there are in the world that share your mindset, find online communities that share your perspective or interest. You may already do this, but take special note of their locations around the world. They will likely be scattered around the world. Though the point of this exercise is to learn to use the internet to find communities of like-minded people, also take note of how few and far in between these people are.

The most underrated skill in seduction is the ability to screen women. You will get old and ugly one day. Don't waste time with soul suckers.

When men learn how to meet and seduce women, they become enamored with their new ability. Going from romantic invisibility to having options with attractive women is one of the best things to happen to a man. It is also extremely intoxicating. It is incredibly easy to go overboard with these new found abilities.

What guys discover is that an increase in quantity does not guarantee an increase in quality. Due to an increase in the number of encounters combined with detrimental societal forces at play, you end up meeting a higher percentage of low-quality women than you would have without improved game.

Sadly, guys never learn how to screen for women that will form wasteful relationships. Guys are generally good at detecting the red flags of craziness, but are terrible at not getting involved with these types of women.

For all of the dedication and discipline that goes into learning to be an attractive man, surprisingly little of it is expended on learning how to control urges that land men with highly questionable women. The most underrated skill in seduction is not just the ability to screen for red flags, but also the discipline to avoid the women with them.

Actionable Advice

Good judgment comes from experience. Getting lots of

experience requires bad judgment. Think about all of the romantic encounters you've had. If your list of flings and relationships is running low, add in girls that you know well enough to make an assessment of their personality.

It doesn't matter if they're single or not. Group the people into three categories: "marriage potential", "dating potential", and "run the hell away from" potential. Base this only on their personality traits.

Once you have the people grouped, take a look at the people in the "run the hell away from". They will have commonalities. You will see these commonalities in every aspect of their personality and appearance.

Mark these down for your future encounters. People are remarkably predictable. Take note of how their behavior corresponds to the flags you track. The consistency you see will go a long way in your ability to screen potential mates.

The best part of being alive now is that we can find other people who are woke. The old days must have been lonely.

Even if you live in the middle of nowhere, the internet makes it possible for you to exchange ideas and meet interesting people from anywhere. You can learn anything you want from any place you want to. You can meet anyone you want to and learn from their experiences first hand. While it can be argued that technology has made people interact less in person, it has also allowed people to form relationships that would have otherwise never occurred.

Nearly everyone today can form their own tribe, even if it's virtual. From there it's only a matter of time before you have friends that you are meeting in person. Though one of the greatest criticism of the internet is that it leads people to antisocial behavior, it has incredible potential to form new relationships of all types.

Actionable Advice

You likely already belong to some type of internet community centered around your interest. If you don't, your goal is to find one. Once you do, your goal is to take on more of a leadership role in the topics you discuss and the ideas put forth. Nurture and grow your community, as it is as much a part of you as you are of it.

Find someone that's perfect for you--Even if they aren't. Especially if you aren't.

This is a poetic way of expressing an empirical fact. People are happiest when they match up with someone within a point of their own level of attractiveness. It assumes that men do most of their assessing (on the 10-point scale) by looks and that women do most of their assessing by personality, status, and income. The happiest couples are those where the woman is as beautiful as the man is successful. You want to find people with your level of imperfection in these metrics to assure maximal stability.

This pairing goes even deeper. Ideally, you want to find people that are at about the same place you are in life, moving the same direction at about the same speed. There are exceptions, but this is the general formula for two people matching well and having timing on their side. What's great about this is that you can always find someone who is where you are in life, trying to get where you are going and will learn with you.

In the end, building a relationship is about finding the best match for you. Not the match with the highest ranking. You want to find someone where you are or is willing to be patient while you catch up.

People can tell a lot about you if they meet your girlfriend first. Your standards speak volumes about your character and self-esteem.

Dating is a marketplace. In this sexual marketplace, each person has a value. The value takes into consideration all of the factors one sex finds attractive in the other. The greater the value one brings to the table, the greater the value of the person they are able to attract. Therefore, one can make a fairly accurate assessment of the quality of a person if they meet their lover first.

The longer the exposure to a partner, the better the guess you can make about the quality of the person's mate. Who you are with speaks volumes about who you are to other people before anything you do or say reveals your character.

Actionable Advice

It is often said that you are the average of the 5 people you spend the most time around. This is correct but it's also just a mathematical convenience. You are also heavily influenced by who you spend the most time around. This not only applies to the person you are committed to but also to the caliber of people that you date. Therefore, this is an excellent opportunity for you to learn about yourself.

Observe the quality of the people you date or the person you are with. Assess their attractiveness. It doesn't matter what the attractiveness of a person once was. What matters is what it is at the moment. This will reveal more about yourself than perhaps you are prepared to confront, but it is a soft way to confront

248

uncomfortable truths about yourself. The quality of the person we are with tells us a great deal about our level as well.

A great number of relationships have been ruined by confusing blunt honesty with unsolicited opinion.

People believe that their opinion is the truth. They treat this truth as if it's a gospel that needs to be delivered, regardless of the circumstance. Truth should never be concealed, but the mistake these people make is confusing opinion with fact. An opinion is merely your perspective on things. It may be based on facts, but the facts will speak for themselves. The opinion you form based on the facts is nothing more than an interpretation. Because it's not a fact, it can neither be right or wrong.

A fact is simply a fact. It is provable by a third party, can be independently replicated and leads to predictions precise enough to be tested. Statements regarding fact can be either true or false. Facts are falsifiable. Opinions are not. Some facts need to be shared. Others are shared for wanton cruelty. There is nothing to gain by the deployment of such facts and truths. But nonetheless, they are facts and as such people have a right to make a decision based on them.

Problems arise when a person shares an opinion and justifies the discomfort caused by claiming to be "telling the truth". This is not only incorrect but unnecessary. By mistakenly referring to an opinion as truth, it's given a false sense of gravity with real potential to do damage. People know their opinions are flimsy—all opinions are flimsy. But when looking to express an unpopular or derisive opinion, doing it under the guise of "just being honest" attempts to bestow upon it a legitimacy that it would otherwise lack.

Actionable Advice

We can improve our ability to communicate by learning to be efficient and accurate. There is a piece of wisdom that says "If you propose to speak, ask yourself if it's true, if it's necessary and if it's kind". Try to make it through one day speaking by this standard and take note of how you feel.

Many of us default to sarcasm in our daily communication. This is nothing more than a defense mechanism. Speaking only true, necessary and kind words will cause you to see just how much of your speech is not designed to contribute, but rather to defend or ridicule.

The Prisoner's Dilemma is a quantitative way to test the loyalty of your friends.

The prisoner's dilemma is a problem that addresses incentives and relationships. There are many versions of it, but the basic idea goes like this: A pair of friends rob a bank, get caught, and are put into separate rooms. They do not know what the other is being told but they are given the option of staying silent or telling the police it was their friend who robbed the bank and they had nothing to do with it. They won't know what the other has chosen until they have made their choice.

If the friends betray each other, they each get two years in jail.
If one betrays the other but the other stays silent, the traitor goes free and the betrayed does 3 years.
If they both remain silent, they only do 1 year in prison.

The original purpose of this experiment was to demonstrate why two people won't cooperate when it might be in their best interest to do so. It certainly accomplishes this, but it also is a test of loyalty. True loyalty is tested only when it is a person's best interest to go against you but they remain by your side. Keep these individuals close, for they will go to hell with you. In doing so, they can make hell seem a little shorter. You end up doing 1 year in prison with a pal instead of 3 years alone.

Actionable Advice

Loyalty is valuable because we know that people make mistakes. If we only followed those who never do wrong, we would descend into anarchy. If you have no one loyal to you, then start by being loyal to someone else. While you can't excuse every mistake that a person makes, it's not difficult to be inspired by someone for the good they do. This will help you understand the value of loyalty.

For a relationship to work two people have to be going in the same direction, at the same speed at the same time.

The following claim isn't scientific. It's merely observation combined with analytics and intuition. The people most likely to remain together in a long-term romantic relationship are people who have the same level and type of ambition about advancing their life. If two people aren't at the same point or improving at approximately the same rate, then one of three things happens.

The most optimistic scenario is that the lagging party speeds up or the advanced party slows down. This works for some, but many aren't willing to take this approach. This means someone either has stifled goals or experiences overwhelming pressure. These are courses of action that lead to feelings of contempt. Contempt is the most poisonous emotion there is in any relationship.

What most often happens is that the partner moving at a faster pace or that's at a different place will get bored and view the other as complacent. The partner that's lagging will get bored and view the other as unavailable. This doesn't mean that the people need to have the same goals, but they do need to be moving towards something that improves their life along metrics that the both members find valuable. This is the secret to long-term happiness in a relationship.

Actionable Advice

This is yet another reason to work at being the best

version of yourself. This is done so that you always have the option of being the patient one in a relationship. This position gives you options and allows you to make decisions in the relationship about the direction you want it to go.

Ideally, you want to be at the same place, at the same time, moving at the same speed. Unfortunately, this is not always possible. The next best thing is to always strive to towards being the most ambitious person you can be. This way you will exercise much greater control over your romantic destiny.

Unconditional love makes you complacent. You should have to earn and maintain the bonds of another person.

Unconditional love is a very dangerous idea. It makes people believe that they don't have to earn the greatest devotion of time a person can make. The only people in this world entitled to unconditional love are a person's children. This is because children are such a huge investment of time and resources. Not only that, but a child is incapable of appreciating the sacrifice of time and resources.

Because an adult can appreciate the amount of time and energy that goes into building a loving relationship, they do not get the benefit of being in a relationship defined by unconditional love. They must do what it takes to remain lovable. Each person must decide what is a violation of love and have the emotional discipline to extinguish a relationship if these violations occur.

Actionable Advice

Decide what your deal breakers are in a relationship. Many people have only a rough idea, but you must take the time sketch out what actions or behaviors you deem intolerable for a person you are involved with. Take the list seriously. This is not your wish list of traits in a partner. This is the list that decides what makes you leave someone after you've formed a partnership. This list determines what you're worth in a relationship by clearly stating what behavior and actions you will not accept if they wish to receive your time.

All dating advice reduces to 1) Ruthlessly enforce standards 2) Increase value to attract quality people. The rest are minor details.

To increase the quality and quantity of people that you attract, you have to be more attractive. This means that you must increase how valuable you are to the people that you want to find you attractive. Assuming that you desire a high caliber of person, you'll have to increase what you bring to the table. People understand this part, for it is painfully obvious.

The part that is more elusive is what happens after you improve your value. Once your value is improved, then you will have a problem managing all of the people that you now attract. If you aren't careful, these situations will inundate you with undesired attention. Once that happens, you will miss out on quality individuals because you are exhausted and annoyed.

To improve the quality of people that you date, you have to screen out individuals that do not meet your standards. As you raise your value, you'll have more people that are interested in you so this skill becomes even more important. Don't just focus on increasing value. Also, focus on how to sort the best from the worst.

Actionable Advice

There is a simple way to screen people. All you have to do is eliminate anyone that is in a worse position than you on any metric. This means don't date anyone in worse shape than you, less intelligent than you, less ambitious, less involved in the world, less family oriented, less whatever.

Your only goal is here to skim down the crowd of suitors that ultimately comes with being a high-quality person. This method of screening isn't shallow, as it means that you'll only be paired with people who are similar to you and thus better able to connect with.

People love novelty. Routine bores them. You've got a better chance of getting what you want being different. At least you'll be remembered.

There is so much stimulus in the world today. Between social media, mainstream media, alternative media, the people you work with and the people you care about, there is hardly any attention left for new things. However, the brain has evolved to believe that new things are good. As a result, most people have the power to be distracted rather easily. This is good if you want to gain the attention of the masses.

For people with developed discipline, getting their attention presents a different problem but the solution is the same. People that are good at shutting out the daily noise are able to do so because they know there is nothing special about it. Getting the attention of these people requires you to be different and unique. After all, they are used to the average person and event. You must be more than that in anything you put effort into.

Actionable Advice

Never downplay what makes you different. Uniqueness is attractive and powerful. People crave familiarity but are seduced by novelty. If you have a hobby, talent or interest that is unique, embrace it fully. Whatever is different about you—be your athletic ability, music talent, interest in the world, or even style of dress, do not conform to the actions of the masses. You will disappear in the noise of them all. Rather, stay true to yourself and what makes you a unique individual. This is how you become a novelty in the world of routines.

Not Caring What Other People Think Is A Super Power

Intense emotional commitment devours your life force. Beware of someone claiming to have been in serious love more than four times under age 30.

An intense emotional relationship requires a great commitment of energy and time. This is true on both the large scale and within the individual. Because of the huge investment in time and energy, each relationship makes it harder to bond in the next one. Human energy is finite. There may be exceptions, but human beings don't seem to be designed for multiple, deep and intense pair bonds.

People who have a large portion of their energy removed (through a few long term intense bonds or several short-term bonds) have a difficult time getting close to anyone. Actually, it becomes impossible to bond not only because of the fundamental changes that happen in the brain but also because they exist in a constant comparison mode. Having many relationships greatly increases the risk of being in a perpetual "grass is greener on the other side" syndrome.

You must also consider the bad judgments and actions that must constantly occur to be in a state of serial relationships or heavy hook up culture. This is not to say that one should stay in their first relationship forever or never have a fling, but if a person isn't learning and becoming a better person from each encounter, then they are becoming worse. This is a simple law of the universe. There is no neutrality—either you are advancing or regressing.

Sober game: If you can meet girls without drinking you are so far ahead in the game of life that other dudes might as well not play.

If you need alcohol to talk to women, the places you can talk to women is mostly limited to happy hour, loud clubs and smoky bars. Your time to meet girls is also extremely limited. Unfortunately, this requires the sacrifice of productive time or time used to recover from other types of hard work.

Since you are drinking, your interactions are going to be ineffective and inefficient. Perhaps the greatest negative is that to avoid involuntary celibacy, you have to carve out chunks of your productive hours to meet women. This makes the interaction worth more than it needs to be, forcing you to focus on the outcome rather than the process.

When you talk to women sober, you have more opportunities. You can still talk to a girl that's drinking because you retain your wit and charm. However, trying to talk to sober women while intoxicated doesn't usually go well.

When you learn to talk to women without alcohol, you see how abundant your selection of women is. The quality of the women you meet will increase because there are some interesting girls that are simply too busy to be bothered with a bar.

You will have almost no competition because 98% of men will not hit on women sober during the day. The ones that try will say something awkward or inappropriate out of nervousness. This means that by being a normal guy that is courageous enough to flirt with a girl, sober during the day, you will be in the 1%. It's only lonely at the top because there isn't any competition. This is a very good thing.

Actionable Advice

Start conversations with girls during daylight hours, sober, and as part of your normal routine. You are not allowed to meet a new girl in a bar either. While you don't have to be anti-social, you are no longer in the business of pursuing romantic opportunities in this environment. Every day, talk to a girl in a sober environment, with the intention of getting a date.

This continues until you are no longer single. We are building a fundamental habit that will improve your life in all areas. You will not only meet more girls, but you will also save a lot of time and energy that would have otherwise been used meeting women at night along with the activities that typically accompany it.

About the Author

You can read more writing at Ed Latimore's Blog at http://www.edlatimore.com.

Connect with Ed Latimore:

Website: http://www.mindandfist.com
Twitter: https://twitter.com/EdLatimore
Facebook:
https://www.facebook.com/EdLatimoreBoxer/
Instagram: EdwardLatimore

There you can get the latests updates and blog posts.

Made in the USA
San Bernardino, CA
08 August 2017